The BUSINESS of HEALING

Robert Medhurst B.Nat.

A GUIDE TO PRACTICE
ESTABISHMENT AND PRACTICE
MANAGEMENT FOR NON-MEDICAL
HEALTHCARE PROFESSIONALS

The Business of Healing.
A guide to practice establishment and practice management for non-medical healthcare professionals.

First published, by the author, 2002.
Reprinted 2003, 2004, 2006 (twice)

ISBN 0-9589798-0-3

Cover design by Robert Medhurst. Printed and bound by Hyde Park Press, Adelaide, South Australia.

For correspondence and the purchase of copies of this book, please contact the author,

Robert Medhurst
PO Box 153
Greenock
SA 5360
0412482228
e-mail- medhurstr@yahoo.com

Disclaimer
This book is intended as a guide only. It is not intended to replace the services of legal or financial advisors, tax agents, marketing advisors or any other professional person whose area of expertise may be discussed herein. At all times the reader should seek the advice of the relevant professional. All financial, taxation, and other figures used here, as well as legislation and regulations, telephone numbers, internet addresses and other contact details are, to the best of the authors knowledge, correct at the time of writing. The accuracy of all of these particulars should be confirmed by the appropriate authorities before acting upon them.

To Katie Behlau for her love, assistance and editing skills, Sonja Brownie for her support and enthusiasm for the teaching of this subject, Andrew Shannon for his financial wizardry, Sally Roberts for her Internet and marketing flair, and to the students over the years who have asked questions and thought of the things that I had not, thank you.

Contents

Introduction
What Makes a Good Practitioner?

There are many things that will determine whether or not a healthcare practitioner is successful. A good working knowledge of the healing arts that one has chosen to pursue, and the means of applying that knowledge are a small part of a broader matrix of skills that will support commercial viability. Success is also reliant upon one's skills in areas such as time management, communication, marketing, finance and strategic thinking. The ability to remain motivated, focused, confident and committed over the long term, is also essential. Along with these aptitudes must go the ability and motivation to remain abreast of developments and responsibilities in the legal, legislative and ethical environments in which we work, as well as the developments in our own branches of healing and the branches that impact on our practice and the lives of our clients.

Managing all of these things, as well as maintaining our own personal lives, can be an enormous task. Whilst the life of a successful healthcare practitioner may not be one that's suited to the faint-hearted, the personal rewards more than compensate for the mental and physical rigours that a busy practice demands.

Why Do You Want to be a Therapist?

For some, it may be the promise of financial reward. For others, the reward may simply be the pleasure inherent in healing. For the majority, the enthusiasm that drives us will be fuelled by a mixture of those things. Either way, this is an essential question to ask because unless we can identify the reason for embarking upon this journey, we have no identifiable goal, and without this we cannot plot the course that our journey must take if we're to make it successful.

It may also be useful to ask yourself whether your professional goals are part of your personal goals, and which is subservient to the other. Many of us, without realising it, wake up one day to find that our professional life has consumed our personal life, and that our personal life no longer exists. Do we want them to be separate entities? Where does one stop and the other begin?

How Long Do You Plan to be a Therapist?

This may seem like an odd question, particularly if you're just embarking upon a clinical practice, but it's an important aspect of several issues, not the least of which is the reason for becoming a therapist in the first place. If operating a practice forms part of an overall personal plan, then one's practice life should conceivably have a definable beginning and a definable end. Therefore a succession plan, consisting of retirement strategies and the transfer of responsibilities for the clients that one has served over the course of the life of the practice, is an essential consideration not just for the health and wellbeing of the practitioner, but the community one serves.

How Do You Stay in Practice?

For a short period of time after you've finished your training and graduated from your chosen institution, you may be sustained by the lingering excitement of finally being unleashed upon the world with a licence to heal, your heart may be filled with the hope of providing salvation to humanity, and you're bursting with anticipation to replicate the miracle cures that you'd heard about in classes at college or university.

This period of hope and confidence may last for some time, after which grim reality starts to set in and it's often at this point that many people feel like giving up. Instituting strategic planning to reach defined goals, measuring and monitoring performance and being proactive in all of the areas that impact upon your business can generate and sustain motivation that will last long after the initial post-graduation enthusiasm has expired.

Among the many issues discussed in this text, these mentioned above should be given serious consideration as they form the crux of much of what will determine whether the practice is successful or otherwise. The aim of this book, and the hope of the author, is that through the chapters that follow you'll acquire information and tools that you'll be able to use to build a structure that will allow you to effectively and efficiently realise your goals.

Suggested Texts:
Money Success and You by John Kehoe, 1991, Zoetic, USA, ISBN 0 9694059 1 X
Getting to Yes by Roger Fisher and William Ury, 1991, Random Century, Australia,
ISBN 0-7126-5087-3
The Medical Interview by Ainslie Meares, Charles C Thomas, USA, 1957
Complementary Medicine: Ethics and Law by Michael Wier, 2000, Prometheus, Australia, ISBN 0-646-39628-5

1. Resources

Throughout this text, mention will be made of the various regulations and requirements that impact upon the operation of a non-medical healthcare practice. The contact details for the organisations that enforce these regulations, as well as the details for those organisations that may be able to offer you support, follow. It should be kept in mind here that whilst these bodies have to balance their objectives between an interest in your commercial viability and the interests of your clients and the community, their ability to assist you with your objectives should never be discounted.

Federal

Australasian Performing Right Association Ltd (APRA)
www.apra.com.au For music licences.
Australian Bureau of Statistics
www.abs.gov.au or 1300 035 070
For publications such as census counts for small areas, social atlases, basic community profiles, household expenditure surveys, business operations and industry performance, profiles of Australian businesses, regional statistics and other demographic data.
Australian Competition and Consumer Commission
www.accc.gov.au
For information on consumer legislation and advice on the sale of products and services.
Australian Government Business Entry Point
132846 or www.business.gov.au For all government services.
Australian Securities and Investments Commission (ASIC).
1300 300 630 or www.asic.gov.au
For information on companies and company formation.
Australian Taxation Office
132869 or www.ato.gov.au
Complementary Healthcare Council (CHC)
0262604022
For information on technical and regulatory issues that affect natural and complementary healthcare providers.
Employment, Workplace Relations and Small Business, Dept of
www.dewrsb.gov.au
For general employment issues and small business advice.
IP Australia
www.ipaustralia.gov.au For patents and trademarks
Job Network
www.jobnetwork.gov.au For information and assistance in the employment of staff.
Phonographic Performance Company of Australia (PPCA)
9th Floor 263 Clarence St Sydney 02-92677877. For music licences.
Therapeutic Goods Administration (TGA)
PO Box 100 Woden ACT 1800 020 653 http://www.health.gov.au/tga
The TGA is a Division of the Federal Department of Health and Aging. It is responsible for administering the provisions of the Therapeutic Goods Act to monitor and regulate the safety, quality and efficacy of therapeutic goods designed for use in humans (medicines and devices) used in Australia including natural and complementary goods and diagnostic devices. The TGA also regulates the labelling and advertising that relate to therapeutic goods.

Wageline
1300655266 or www.wagenet.gov.au
For information on awards, leave, dismissal and workplace agreements.
For state offices of some of these departments, see individual state entries.

South Australia
Australasian Performing Right Association Ltd (APRA)
Suite 54, 55 Melbourne St North Adelaide 08-8239 2222 www.apra.com.au
Australian Bureau of Statistics
Commonwealth Centre 55 Currie St Adelaide 08- 8237 7555
Australian Competition and Consumer Commission
13 Grenfell St Adelaide- 08-82054350
Australian Securities and Investments Commission (ASIC)
Level 8 100 Pirie St Adelaide 08-8202 8500
Australian Taxation Office
91 Weymouth St Adelaide 132861
Business Enterprise Centres
131891 www.tbc.sa.gov.au
These are regionally based business advice centres- check the White Pages
telephone directory for the nearest location.
Business Licensing
08-84633850
Child and Youth Health, Dept of
295 South Terrace Adelaide 08-83031500 www.cyh.sa.gov.au
For parents and children's health issues.
Consumer and Business Affairs, Dept of
Chesser House 91-97 Grenfell St Adelaide 08-82049533, 131882
www.ocba.sa.gov.au
For business registration and licensing, retail and commercial tenancies.
Employment, Workplace Relations and Small Business, Dept of
3rd Floor, KPMG House, 115 Grenfell St Adelaide 08-83030400
Health and Aged Care, Dept of
55 Currie St Adelaide 08-82378111
For information on Medicare levies, mental health and general public health
issues.
Industry and Trade, Dept of
Terrace Towers 178 North Tce Adelaide 08-83032400
For general advice on employment issues.
IP Australia
1 King William St Adelaide 1300 651 010
Law Society of South Australia
124 Weymouth St Adelaide 0882319972 www.lssa.asn.au
For referral to lawyers and legal advice (charges are applied for the latter).

Mental Health Services
131465- 24 hr emergency centre. For advice on suicide etc.
Office of the Small Business Advocate
74 South Terrace Adelaide 08-82216120 or 1800 240489 www.osba.on.net
For assistance with problems relating to government services.
SA Employers Chamber of Commerce and Industry
136 Greenhill Rd Unley- 08-83731422 www.abol.net/saecci
SA Government website
www.sa.gov.au
Small Business Training Centre
120 Currie St Adelaide 08-84100000
www.tafe.sa.au/institutes/adelaide/sbtc/sbtc.html
This organisation operates workshops on business skills and business management
and provides general business advice.
Super SA
200 Victoria Square (East) Adelaide 1300 369315 www.supersa.gov.a.au
For all superannuation advice.
Superannuation Guarantee Coordinator
ATO- 131020
WorkCover Corporation
100 Weymouth St Adelaide 08-82332222, 131855 www.WorkCover.sa.gov.au
For all WorkCover issues.
Workplace Services, Dept of
08-83030400 1300 365255 www.Eric.sa.gov.au
For dismissal information and advice on workplace safety, occupational health
and safety.

New South Wales
Australasian Performing Right Association Ltd (APRA)
6 -12 Atchison St St Leonards 02-9935 7900
Australian Bureau of Statistics
Level 5 St Andrews House Sydney Square Sydney (George St, next to Sydney
Town Hall) 02-9268 4111
Australian Securities & Investments Commission (ASIC)
Level 8/ 55 Market St Sydney 02-9911 2500
Business Licensing Information Service (BLIS)
1800463976 or 02-96198722 For information on business licensing.
Community Services, Dept of, Helpline
132111
        Child Abuse Prevention Services 1800 688 009

Fair Trading, Dept of
1 Fitzwilliam St Parramatta 02- 9895 0111 13 3220 www.fairtrading.nsw.gov.au
For rental tenancy information, business names registration, business licensing, consumer and trader information on goods and services. Also see White Pages telephone directory listings for regional centres.
Health and Aging, Dept of
1800 048998 For general public health issues.
Industrial Relations, Dept of
0292438774 or 132005 For general employment advice.
IP Australia
Level 1 45 Clarence St Sydney 1300 651 010
Law Society of NSW
170 Phillip St Sydney 02-9926 0333 www.lawsocnsw.asn.au
For referral to legal services
NSW Government website
www.nsw.gov.au
State and Regional Development, Dept of
131145 or www.smallbiz.nsw.gov.au
Operates the Small Business Advisory Centres- see website for details of regional offices which run workshops on business skills, management, marketing and advertising for small business.
Superannuation Guarantee Coordinator
2 Meredith St Bankstown 131020
WorkCover Corporation
400 Kent Street Sydney 02 9370 5000

Western Australia
Australasian Performing Right Association (APRA)
177a York St Subiaco 08-9382 8299
Australian Bureau of Statistics
 2 The Esplanade Perth 08-93605323
Australian Competition and Consumer Commission
233 Adelaide Terrace Perth 08-93253266
Australian Securities and Investments Commission (ASIC).
Level 1, 66 St Georges Terrace Perth 08-92614200
Business Enterprise Centre
08-93253388 or 1800 093340
For small business assistance. See the White Pages telephone directory for all metropolitan and regional listings.
Business Licence and Information Centre
553 Hay St Perth 08-92200235
For information on business licences.
Chamber of Commerce and Industry
180 Hay St East Perth 08-93657555

Employment, Workplace Relations and Small Business, Dept of
250 St Georges Terrace Perth 08-94644200
Health Dept of Western Australia
189 Royal St East Perth 08-92224222
For information on mental health, suicide etc.
Industry, Science and Resources, Dept of
28 The Esplanade Perth 08-93279500 For advice on business development.
IP Australia
233 Adelaide Tce Perth 1300 651 010
Law Society of Western Australia
33 Barrack St Perth 08-92213222 For referral to legal services
Ministry of Fair Trading
219 St Georges Terrace Perth 08-92820777
For small business registration, business names, consumer and business affairs etc.
Productivity and Labour Relations, Dept of
2 Havelock St West Perth 08-92227700
For information on employment issues.
Small Business, Dept of
19th Floor 197 St Georges Terrace Perth 08-92229699
Small Business Development Corporation
553 Hay St Perth 08-92200235 For general advice on small business.
WA Government website
www.wa.gov.au
WorkCover Western Australia
2 Bedbrook Place Shenton Park 08-93885555 or www.WorkCover.wa.gov.au

Queensland
Australasian Performing Right Association (APRA)
168 Barry Pde Fortitude Valley 07-3257 1007
Australian Bureau of Statistics
313 Adelaide St Brisbane 07-32226022
Australian Competition and Consumer Commission
500 Queen St Brisbane 07-38354666 or 1300302502 or www.accc.gov.au
Australian Securities & Investments Commission (ASIC)
Level 20/ 240 Queen St Brisbane 07-3867 4900
Business Licensing- Smartlicence
400 Boundary St Spring Hill 07-32211620 or 1800061631
Employment and Training, Dept of
75 William St Brisbane 07-32252416 or 1300369925 or www.det.qld.gov.au
For general employment advice.
Employment, Workplace Relations and Small Business, Dept of
215 Adelaide St Brisbane 07-32231250 or www.dewrsb.qld.gov.au
Families, Dept of
111 George St Brisbane 07-32248045 or www.families.qld.gov.au

For advice on child abuse and other issues. See details for regional centres in the White Pages telephone directory.

Industrial Relations, Dept of
75 William St Brisbane 1300369945 or www.dir.qld.gov.au
For advice on awards, leave and dismissal issues.

IP Australia
Level 1, 102 Adelaide St Brisbane 07-32291304

Law Society of Queensland
179 Ann St Brisbane 07-38425888
For referral to legal services

Qld Government website
www.qld.gov.au

Queensland Health
147-163 Charlotte St Brisbane 07-32340680
For mental health and other health issues.

State Development, Dept of
100 George St Brisbane 07-32248568 or www.statedevelopment.qld.gov.au
For advice on operating small businesses in Queensland.

Tourism, Racing and Fair Trading, Dept of
111 George St Brisbane 07-32461500 or www.dtrft.qld.gov.au
For business names registration, consumer and business affairs issues.

WorkCover Queensland
1300 362 128

ACT
ACT Government website
www.act.gov.au

ACT WorkCover
North Bldg London Circuit Canberra City 02-6205 0200

Australian Bureau of Statistics
ABS House 5 Benjamin Way Belconnen ACT 02- 6252 5000

Australian Competition & Consumer Commission
470 Northbourne Ave Dickson 02- 6243 1111

Australian Securities & Investments Commission (ASIC)
5th Floor 15 London Cct Canberra City 02-6250 3850

Business Training Advisory Board (ACT) Inc
Andrew Arcade 42 Giles St Kingston 02- 6295 2353
For assistance with business skills.

Employment and Workplace Relations, Dept of
Garema Court 148-180 City Walk Canberra ACT 02-6121 6000

Fair Trading, Dept of
110 -112 Monaro St Queanbeyan 02- 6299 3433 13 3220
www.fairtrading.nsw.gov.au For consumer and trader information & complaints, business licences, rental and tenancy information.

IP Australia
47 Bowes St Phillip 02-6283 2999 or 1300 651 010
Law Society of the ACT
1 Farrell Pl Canberra City 02- 6247 5700
For referral to legal services.

Tasmania
Australian Bureau of Statistics
200 Collins St Hobart 03-62225999
Australian Competition and Consumer Commission
86 Collins St Hobart 03-62159333
Australian Securities & Investments Commission (ASIC)
Level 2/ 66 -80 Collins St Hobart 03-6235 6850
Employment, Workplace Relations and Small Business, Dept of
188 Collins St Hobart 03-62226303
Dept of Consumer and Business Affairs, Dept of
15 Murray St Hobart 1300654499
For consumer affairs and fair trading, business registration and business names registration.
Health and Family Services, Dept of
34 Davey St Hobart 03-62307650
For child abuse complaints, child and family services.
Law Society of Tasmania
28 Murray St Hobart 03-62344133
For referral to legal services.
Southern Mental Health Services
St John Ave New Town 03-62307549
For mental health services, suicide etc.
State Development, Dept of
Business Licence Information Service- 1800 005 262
For business licences.
Tasmanian Government website
www.tas.gov.au
WorkCover
See Dept of Infrastructure Energy & Resources, 10 Murray Street Hobart 7000
300 366 322, 03-6233 7657 or www.dier.tas.gov.au
See white pages listing for regional area contact details for all of these resources.

Victoria
Australasian Performing Right Association (APRA)
3 -5 Sanders Pl Richmond 03-9426 5200
Australian Bureau of Statistics
Level 6 CU Tower 485 Latrobe St Melbourne 03-96157000

Australian Securities & Investments Commission (ASIC)
Level17 485 Latrobe St Melbourne 03-9280 3500
Business Licensing Authority
Level 2 452 Flinders St Melbourne 03-96276299
For information on business licensing.
Consumer and Business Affairs, Dept of
452 Flinders St Melbourne 03-96276000
For information on business names, consumer and tenancy issues.
Health and Aged Care, Dept of
Casseldon Place, 2 Lonsdale St Melbourne 03-9658888
For general public health issues.
Human Services, Dept of
555 Collins St Melbourne 03-96167777.
For information on child abuse services.
Industrial Relations, Dept of
1 Macarthur St Melbourne 03-96515560 or www.vic.gov.au/ir
For general employment advice.
IP Australia
565 Bourke St Melbourne 1300 651 010
Law Institute of Victoria
GPO Box 263C Melbourne 03-96079311.
For referral to legal services.
State and Regional Development, Dept of
55 Collins St Melbourne 03-96519999
Operates the Small Business Advisory Centres- see website for details of regional
offices which run workshops on business skills, management, marketing and
advertising for small business. See also www.sbv.viv.gov.au
Victorian Government website
www.vic.gov.au
WorkCover Corporation
222 Exhibition St Melbourne 03-96411555

Northern Territory
Asian Relations, Dept of
76 The Esplanade, Darwin 08-89995153
For business names registration and business licences.
Australian Bureau of Statistics
81 Smith St Darwin 08-9432111
Australian Competition and Consumer Commission
9-11 Cavanagh St Darwin 08-89431499
Australian Securities & Investments Commission (ASIC)
Darwin Harbour View Plaza Level 5 8 McMinn St Darwin 08-8943 0950
Business Enterprise Centre 23 Albatross Winnellie 08-8922 9529

For small business advice. Also see White Pages telephone directory for all regional centres or call 1800 229 500.

Child and Family Protective Services
08-89227111. For advice on child and family health issues.

Consumer and Business Affairs
66 The Esplanade, Darwin 08-89995184
For all consumer product and service advice.

Employment, Workplace Relations and Small Business, Dept of
80 Mitchell St Darwin 08-9365000.

Fair Trading, Dept of- Dept of Justice
45 Mitchell Street Darwin 08-8999 6047 www.justice.nt.gov.au
For small business registration.

Industries and Business, Dept of
Development House, The Esplanade, Darwin 08-9244200 or www.tbc.nt.gov.au
For general business issues.

Law Society of the Northern Territory
22 Mitchell St Darwin 08-89815104.
For referral to legal services.

Northern Territory Government website
www.nt.gov.au

Small Business Advisory Services Development House
The Esplanade, Darwin 08-9997914. For general small business advice.
See White Pages telephone directory listing for regional area contact details for all of these resources.

2. The Costs of Operating the Business
Establishment Costs
Before delving too far into the activities related to setting up a practice, it's useful to be aware of the costs involved in setting it up. What follows is the estimated cost of doing this. It does not take into account any internal building work, painting, air conditioning or heating, expensive reception desks, design costs for business cards, brochures, advertisements or other marketing material, chiropractic or osteopathic treatment tables, homoeopathic computer software or any other specialist items. Note that no allowance for working capital is included here, nor is any allowance made for the costs (travel and phone etc) involved in acquiring these items. Pamphlets rather than brochures are listed here – it is suggested that pamphlets be used as direct mail marketing tools as a more effective means of getting the practice started than brochures and are considerably cheaper to have printed (more will be said on this later).

The Business of Healing

The establishment costs may consist of the following.

Item	Estimated cost
Business name registration	$109
Association membership (example used is ATMS Professional Membership)	$145
Insurance (total package through broker)	$1000
Bond and stamp duty	$1300
Electricity deposit	$83
Telephone connection (if line is present and intact)	$55
Examination/massage table	$250
Computer, fax, printer and software (MYOB First Accounts or Quicken)	$3500
Consulting room chair for practitioner	$150
Consulting room chairs (3)	$250
Consulting room desk	$300
Reception desk	$300
Reception chairs (5)	$250
Waiting room table/magazine rack	$100
Filing cabinet (metal 2 drawer)	$150
Desk lamp	$50
First aid kit (St Johns Ambulance kit)	$120
Telephone answering machine	$80
Curtains/blinds	$250
Professional library	$500
Business cards (1000 single sided plain card one colour)	$89
Pamphlets (1000 single side, fold down, A4, single colour, including folding)	$170
Signs	$250
Yellow pages ad (41x14mm reverse block)	$1000
Massage oils	$250
Stationary	$150
Sundries	$250
Dispensary (herbs, homoeopathics and nutritional products)	$5000
Stethoscope	$50
Sphygmomanometer	$150
Measuring cylinders	$50
Empty bottles, caps and printed labels	$230
Total	$16581

Finance Options
Having identified the basic costs involved in setting up the practice, if these establishment costs cannot be met from personal funds, finance may need to be arranged to cover them. There are several options here- short, medium and long term, depending upon how quickly one is able to repay the interest and principle on the loan. The success of the application for finance will depend upon one's ability to present the proposed clinic as a good investment, capable of repaying the loan in the allotted time. A business plan is the best method of making this presentation. This will be discussed later.

Short Term Finance Options
Overdraft- this is normally arranged through a bank, it may need to be negotiated with the bank, and the interest rates will normally be around one percent higher than the standard mortgage rate. The amount of funds available here may be limited, the interest is calculated on the daily outstanding balance, and charged quarterly.

Commercial bill- this is a loan made for a period of 30 to 180 days, and the loan must be paid in full by the due date. The interest rates vary but may be less than the overdraft rate.

Medium Term Finance Options
Personal loan- from a bank or other lending institution, these are made for a fixed period, e.g. five or ten years, and the interest charged is normally about three percent above the standard mortgage rate.

Leasing- under this arrangement, a finance company buys the items in question and then and one leases them over a fixed period. At the end of this period, one then owns these items, and the lease payments are tax deductible.

Long Term Finance Options
Home loan attached personal loan- on a weekly or monthly repayment basis, this may be one of the cheapest options. Interest is paid at the standard mortgage rate but one must have a pre-existing mortgage and have sufficient equity in the property for the lending institution to extend the loan. There are often little or no fees or set up costs and the length of time required to pay the loan is the same as the length of the mortgage.

Bank Investment Loan- these involve an investment by the bank in the business and are available at an interest rate that may be the same as the standard overdraft rate. It should be understood here that banks are relatively conservative institutions, and the business plan one presents for this type of loan needs to be convincing, comprehensive and competently produced.

Investor Finance- this involves investment in your business using money held in trust or investments funds accounts operated by solicitors or accountants. The contact details for those looking to invest can often be found in the classified sections of the major daily newspapers, and the interest rates will vary.

Taking on a Business Partner- it may be that you've formed a limited liability company as a means of running the clinic, in which case it's a relatively easy matter to sell shares in the company to an outside investor, essentially making them a partner in the business in exchange for a certain level of return on their investment. The prospective partner may be a medical practitioner, pharmacist, health food store owner or other person with some experience in healthcare, and who will benefit directly by referring people to the clinic. This individual may well have a good level of business experience, which will also be useful. The sale of shares in the company should be arranged by a solicitor. One may also wish to pursue the option of advertising for a partner in the classified sections of major daily newspapers.

Operating Costs

Having determined how much it will cost to set up the practice, one then needs to know the probable extent of weekly outgoings, and more importantly, how many clients one will have to see to meet these costs (also known as break even) and how many more will have to be seen if one is to generate an income. The figures that follow do not consider the costs of cleaning, the depreciation on items such as stock, computers or other depreciable items, loan fees or staff training. They also ignore dispensary items and dispensary stock as the mark up on these items should make them self-funding.

Item	Weekly cost
Stationary	$10
Textbook upgrades	$10
Association memberships	$5
Insurance	$20
Professional journals	$5
Electricity	$15
Telephone	$30
Rent	$250
Marketing (local newspaper advertising, Yellow Pages advertising, business cards, pamphlets)	$75
Continuing professional education (seminars, conferences etc, for CPE points to maintain professional membership)	$25

Cost of original investment @10% interest invested (it's normal practice to impute the amount that is not being received if one had invested the original establishment cost in an interest bearing instrument)	$30
Total outlay per week, without receptionist	$560
Total outlay per week, with receptionist (costed at $600 per week)	$1160

Break Even
From the figures above, if one considers that the average income per client, including income from therapeutic goods sale, was $50 and a receptionist wasn't employed, one would need to see 12 clients per week.

If employing a receptionist (note that the $600 per week estimate includes salary and on-costs) one would need to see 24 clients per week to beak even.

Generating an Income
If a gross income (that is, without considering tax, superannuation or any other deductions) of $50,000 per year was desired and the practitioner were to take 2 weeks holiday per year, one would need to see 32 clients per week, if a receptionist were not employed. At this income, if a receptionist was employed, 44 clients would need to be seen per week.

It also needs to be kept in mind that it may take 3 to 12 months from start-up before one is seeing a sufficient number of clients to break even, and so cash reserves need to be adequate to meet the requirements that arise during this period. However, the first years cost of many of the things apart from the receptionists' salary will have been covered by the establishment costs.

3. Legal, Statutory Requirements and Other Responsibilities
Associations
For many purposes it's mandatory, and in all cases very useful, to belong to a professional association. For a relatively small fee, the benefits of membership are manifold. Regular seminars and conferences, journals or newsletters, discounts on insurance and advertising as well as the credibility afforded by professional membership, are just a few of the advantages offered by professional associations. Some of these associations are state based, and several have representation in every state in Australia. It may be advantageous to belong to at least one nationally based association, and at least one state based specialist association, as the latter can offer local experience and assistance that may be unobtainable from the larger national associations.

Most professional associations also have the capacity to issue Therapeutic Goods Administration (TGA) advertising exemption certificates. One of the functions of the TGA is to regulate and administer the laws that relate to the advertising of therapeutic goods. Depending upon the therapeutic claims made for these goods and their potential effects, some are allowed for retail sale, and some are restricted to health care professionals. The TGA define health care professionals as properly trained and professionally recognised medical practitioners, dentists, veterinarians, medical specialists, registered nurses, chiropractors, osteopaths, pharmacists, herbalists, naturopaths, homoeopaths, acupuncturists and psychologists. These advertising exemption certificates identify the holder as a member of one of these groups, and normally (although some practitioners have managed to obtain certificates without belonging to an association), only members of those nominated groups have access to the restricted advertising.

In all cases it's useful to contact the appropriate association and ask them what kinds of services they offer to members, and choose the one that best suits your requirements. Most associations offer general or professional membership. General membership may be available to those without professional qualifications but who have an interest in the modalities that relate to the association. Professional membership is available to those who have the appropriate qualifications and clinical experience (see individual associations for these requirements). Applications for professional membership to some associations may also call for photographs of both the practitioner and the clinic in which they practice, as well as character references.

Many associations impose a continuing professional education (CPE) program on their professional members, requiring the accrual of a certain number of CPE points per year. These points are gained by attending approved seminars and conferences or through participation in other approved professional educational activities. The renewal of annual professional membership may be dependent upon the accumulation of the requisite number of points.

General Natural Therapies Associations
Australian Natural Therapists Association (ANTA)
      Total membership- Unknown
      Benefits
            Subsidised professional indemnity insurance
            Practitioner referral service
            Subsidised Yellow Pages advertising
            Skills update seminars
            National accreditation
            Healthcare provider status with most major healthcare insurers
            Complimentary stationary
            Association journal

Fees (full professional membership as ANTA Fellow) per annum
$165 rising to $495 at the third year of membership plus a $110
application fee for the first year.

Contact

National- ANTA PO Box 657 Marrochydore QLD
www.anta.com.au 1800 817577 or see the Yellow Pages
telephone directory entries under Naturopaths in each capital
city

Australian Naturopathic Practitioners Association (ANPA)

Total membership- Unknown

Benefits

National accreditation
Healthcare provider status with many major healthcare insurers
Subsidised professional indemnity insurance
Subsidised Yellow Pages advertising
Association journal

Fees (full professional membership) per annum $253 plus a $50
application fee plus GST for the first year.

Contact

National- ANPA 609-611 Camberwell Rd Camberwell, VIC
03-98890334

Australian Traditional Medicine Society (ATMS)

Total membership- 6398 members

Benefits

Subsidised professional indemnity insurance
Practitioner referral service
Subsidised Yellow Pages advertising
Skills update seminars
National accreditation
Healthcare provider status with most major healthcare insurers
Association journal

Fees (full professional membership) per annum $145 plus GST
and a $50 application fee for the first year.

Contact

National- 12/27 Bank St Meadowbank, NSW 02-98096800 or
see the Yellow Pages telephone directory entries under
Naturopaths in each capital city.

Complementary Medicine Association (CMA)
> Total membership- 600 members
> Benefits
>> Subsidised professional indemnity insurance
>> Subsidised Yellow Pages advertising
>> Skills update seminars
>> National accreditation
>> Healthcare provider status with many major healthcare insurers
>> Association journal
> Fees (full professional membership) per annum $220 plus a $40 application fee for the first year.
> Contact
>> National- CMA PO Box 6412 Baulkham Hills Business Centre, Baulkham Hills, NSW, 1800 117766 www.atms.com.au or see the Yellow Pages telephone directory entries under Naturopaths in each capital city

Specialist Associations
A number of national associations exist to meet the needs of involved in specialised healthcare areas.
Acupuncture
Australian Acupuncture and Chinese Medicine Association (AACMA)
> Total membership- Unknown
> Benefits
>> National referral service
>> National accreditation
>> BAS and GST accounting assistance
>> Concessions on clinic supplies and books
>> Access to seminar videotape library
>> Regular newsletters
>> Research grants
>> Subsidised professional indemnity insurance
>> Free Acupuncture Ethics and Standards Organisation (AESO) membership
>> Healthcare provider status with most major healthcare insurers
> Fees (full professional membership) per annum $195 for new graduates in the first year rising to $495 for subsequent years plus a $165 application fee for the first year.
> Contact-
>> National- AACMA PO Box 5142 West End Qld 1800 025 334 www.acupuncture.org.au

Herbal Medicine
The National Herbalists Association of Australia (NHAA)
 Total membership- 1850
 Benefits
   National referral service
   Regular newsletters
   Healthcare provider status with many major healthcare insurers
   Regular seminars
 Fees (full professional membership) $220 plus a $30 application fee for
  the first year.
 Contact
   National- NHAA, 33 Reserve St Annandale NSW
   02-95607077 www.nhaa.org.au

Homoeopathy
The Australian Homoeopathic Association (AHA)
 Total membership- Unknown
 Benefits
   National referral service
   Clinical mentor program
   Subsidised professional indemnity insurance
   Subsidised Yellow Pages advertising
   Regular newsletters
   Healthcare provider status with many major healthcare insurers
   Regular seminars
 Fees (full professional membership) $220 plus a $33 application fee, fees
  reduced for recent graduates.
 Contact
   National- Jude Cresswell (President) Sydney College of
   Homoeopathic Medicine, 92-94 Norton St Leichhardt
   02 95646731 or 0416298966. http://www.homeopathyoz.org

Chiropractic
The Chiropractors Association of Australia (CAA)
 Total membership- 1800
 Benefits
   National referral service
   Brochure service
   Regular journals
   Discounted general and professional indemnity insurance
   Discounts on some credit card fees provided by some banks
   Healthcare provider status with most major healthcare insurers
   Regular seminars

Connection with government departments such as Veterans
Affairs
CAA support for public awareness campaigns
Fees (full professional membership) per annum $1194.60 with
concessions for recent graduates or new graduates.
Contact
See the entries under Chiropractors in the Yellow Pages
telephone directory for the contact details of the CAA in each
state.

Osteopathy
The Australian Osteopathic Association (AOA)
Total membership- 700
Benefits
National referral service
Access to comprehensive library
Regular journals and newsletters
National locum register
Discounted general and professional indemnity insurance
Discounts on some credit card fees provided by some banks
Healthcare provider status with most major healthcare insurers
Regular seminars
Connection with government departments such as Veterans
Affairs
AOA support for public awareness campaigns
Fees (full professional membership) per annum $815.00 with
concessions for recent graduates or new graduates, plus a joining
fee of $165.00.
Contact
AOA, PO Box 242 Thornleigh NSW 02-94402511 or see
the entries under Osteopaths in the Yellow Pages telephone
directory for the contact details of the AOA in each state.

Massage
The Association of Massage Therapists Australia (AMTA)
Total membership- 1600
Benefits
National referral service
Regular newsletter
Discounted general and professional indemnity insurance
Healthcare provider status with many major healthcare insurers
Discounted Yellow Pages telephone directory advertising
Connection with government departments such as WorkCover
and Comcare

Fees (full professional membership) per annum $187, plus a $75
   application fee, $20 fee for membership certificate and badge,
   and GST of $26.50. Reductions apply for recent graduates.
Contact
   AMTA PO Box 358 Prahran Victoria 03-95103930 or
   www.amta.asn.au

For state based specialist associations, and national associations focused on
specialist areas that do not have a national office, see their entries under the
modality heading in Yellow Pages telephone directory.

Government Regulations
A clinic needs to be able to do 3 things:
* Satisfy the needs of the practitioner
* Satisfy the needs of the clients
* Satisfy the needs of the community by meeting all government regulations
  and requirements

If the clinic cannot meet the needs of the community, it simply won't be able to
operate. Therefore, one needs to be aware of all of the rules and regulations that
apply to the operation of a non-medical healthcare clinic.

In all circumstances you should ensure that you can do what you plan to do in
the area where you want to do it, and that you have written clearance to do so by
local government before you invest any time or money in the establishment of
your business. Local councils have considerable power over the activities of the
businesses that operate within their geographical boundaries. Clearance to
practice may be subject to zoning laws, as well as a development application, and
development application forms should be sought from the local council. The
application will incur an administrative cost of somewhere between $50 and $100
and may take several weeks for the local council to process.

You should also ensure that your business complies with the local ordinances that
apply to health and fire, skin penetration and any other relevant acts. The
council should be consulted in regard to this, and they may refer you to
specialised local utilities or state departments.

Your business may also be subject to regulations that relate to parking and toilet
requirements. These will vary from council to council but you are generally
required to have at least one toilet, and you may have to ensure that adequate
parking is available for every staff member and every person likely to be in the
clinic at the one time. If you plan on erecting a new building there are a large
number of other regulations you'll need to comply with. Once again, the fact that

your business complies with these regulations should be obtained in writing. It is unwise to rely on verbal clearances in any of these circumstances.

Music Licences
If you play music in your clinic- in the waiting room, on your telephone whilst callers are on hold, or by any other means, you'll need to obtain music licences. There are two forms of music licence that one needs to acquire. The first of these comes from the Phonographic Performance Company of Australia (PPCA). This organisation protects the rights of the artist and the recording company. The annual licence fee is between $50 and $60 dollars, and it permits the licence holder to broadcast music into a space with a maximum floor space of one hundred and forty square metres. The second licence needs to be acquired from the Australian Performing Right Association (APRA) which charges an annual fee of between $50 and $100. APRA protects the rights of the music copyright holder. The contact details for APRA can be found in the local White Pages telephone directory.

Treatable and Non-treatable Complaints
Unless one holds the appropriate medical qualifications, non-medical healthcare providers are not legally able to treat cancer, diabetes, aids, epilepsy, hepatitis, leukemia, multiple sclerosis, polio or tuberculosis, a serious communicable disease or HIV AIDS. If you suspect a client suffers from any of these conditions, you must refer them to a medical practitioner for assessment and treatment. You may be able to assist with these conditions as long as the case is overseen by a person with the appropriate medical qualifications. If you don't hold these qualifications, it may only be possible for you to treat clients general state of health. These regulations may not apply in all states of Australia; for example in Queensland, some of these restrictions may not apply. It should be noted that a written disclaimer signed by a client who suffers from one of these conditions does not necessarily defeat these restrictions.

Claims to Cure
In most circumstances you cannot lay claim to the capacity to cure disease, although you may be able to claim the capacity to aid recovery. No guarantees in this regard should ever be given- if you do make these types of assurances and they are not fully realised, you may be subject to a legal claim of liability in contract.

WorkCover
Some members of the non-medical healing professions, such as masseurs, chiropractors, physiotherapists and osteopaths, may be able to provide therapeutic services that are rebatable under the WorkCover scheme for the clients whose treatment is being subsidised under this scheme. The ability to do this requires the acquisition of a WorkCover provider number. The granting of this provider

status involves approval by a WorkCover assessor. The assessor will report to the WorkCover authority on the practitioners suitability in the areas of client management, report writing, clinic surrounds and conditions, and the practitioners understanding of the legal and ethical issues related to such things as consent, discrimination, and confidentiality.

Dispensing Requirements

If dispensing medicines, one needs to be aware of the regulations that pertain to this activity. The TGA govern the regulations related to the labelling of therapeutic goods under their Therapeutic Goods Order Number 48 section 3 (1). Most health care professionals (as defined by the TGA) are exempt from these regulations, but one should still be guided by them, and failure to do this may be viewed rather dimly by a court. In addition to this, any improperly labelled product may be deemed by the Trade Practices Act to be defective and therefore unsuitable for sale. Section 3 (1) of the TGA labelling order mentioned above states (in part) that labels should be firmly and permanently fixed to the container holding the goods, the label text should be in English with characters not less than 1.5mm high. The label should clearly state the nature of the contents, the dose instructions (names rather than numbers must be used here), the manufacturers (the practitioner and clinic) details, expiry date and batch number. For the purpose of dispensing prescribed medicines, the label should also carry the clients' name and date. Any pre-packed products should also be over-labelled in the stated manner.

The label may look like this:

The Herbal Mixture 4.5.02	
Dose instructions: Take 5ml in a little water three times a day	
Client name: Maude Culpepper	Batch number: 104419
	Expiry date: 4.5.03
The Happy Herbalist Norman Happy DBM. 10 Helianthus Drive Happy Hill Qld 4006 Ph/Fax 07-31190004 Prov. No. J99904A ABN 99 777 001 555 www.happy.com.au	

The expiry date should be the earliest date of any of the ingredients used in the product. For example, if one were dispensing a mixture of fluid extracts of the herbs, Echinacea, Calendula and Hydrastis, which had expiry dates of July 2005, August 2006 and May 2005 respectively, the expiry date of the mixture would be May 2005. Labels pre-printed with the practitioners and clinic details, with spaces allocated for the other information required, are commonly used for this purpose, are relatively cheap, convey a professional approach to dispensing and save dispensing time. Further issues on dispensing will be discussed later.

Commercial Entities

A number of options exist that allow business to be conducted through an entity that is legally separate from the practitioner. Some of these entities can:

- Provide the practitioner with the ability to be removed from direct liability for claims that may be made on the business.
- They may allow a sharing of that liability.
- They can provide the opportunity for financial and other input from individuals who are not directly involved in the practice.
- They can provide a means of reducing tax liability.

There are several forms of commercial entities used by non-medical healthcare providers.

Limited Liability Company

This is one of the more popular options if you plan to be in full time practice and are aiming for success. It's a useful means of attracting outside investors and the current taxation structure makes it suitable for minimising the tax burden. This structure requires one or more directors, a secretary and shareholders. The structure should be set up by a solicitor experienced in such matters, and the establishment costs may run to between one and three thousand dollars. It may take up to six weeks to set the company structure in place.

The means by which the company operates should be set out in the "articles of association", which outline the duties and responsibilities of all office bearers, and the method by which profits are distributed. Maintaining the paperwork involved in the operation of a limited liability company can be fairly time consuming, and the company accounts must be audited annually by a chartered public accountant. The company requires its own tax file number, business name and Australian Business Number (ABN) and must be registered with the Australian Securities and Investments Commission (ASIC).

The practitioner may either be an employee of the company, paying tax at the personal tax rate, or may be appointed as a director and shareholder of the company and may be paid dividends. These may be taxed at less than this rate through a system known as franking, which involves some of the tax being covered by the taxation paid by the company. Company earnings made in excess of these dividends may be paid into things such as superannuation which attract a lower rate of tax.

Any debts incurred by the company remain the responsibility of the company rather than the practitioner, and although directors may be sued for those debts, this process is generally more difficult that suing the practitioner directly.

The Business of Healing

Partnership

This is generally a union consisting of two or more individuals. Given that one or more of the partners may have prior business experience and or funds they're willing to invest in the practice, a partnership allows for a wider pool of capital and expertise than would normally be accessible to a sole trader. Each partner is assigned a share in the business, and those shares may be bought or sold. Statistics have shown that partnerships have a high rate of failure, possibly due to disagreements between partners regarding the operation of the business. All partners are jointly liable for debts incurred by the business, or any of the partners, regardless of the extent of the holdings of each partner. For example, in a structure consisting of three partners, two owning ninety percent of the business and the remaining partner owning ten percent, debts incurred by the business will be equally apportioned, that is, each partner will be responsible for one third of the debt.

The partnership should operate under a business name and all partners must be active participants of the business. A tax number must be acquired by the business and each partner pays tax at a rate normally attributable to a sole trader. Income assignment and other matters related to the running of the business must be documented in a partnership agreement, and the agreement should be drafted by an experienced solicitor.

Sole Trader

This is the structure most frequently used by non-medical healthcare practitioners. It's relatively easy to set up and requires minimal cost, and if you wish to cease trading or change the methods of operation in any way, the permission of other parties isn't required. There may also be scope to offset losses that may be incurred by your business in the first year of operation against other sources of income, thereby reducing the total tax burden for that year. Tax is paid at the personal tax rate, an ABN must be acquired and it's preferable to acquire a business name.

As a sole trader your ability to expand is limited by the amount of your own funds and any that you borrow, and if your business is sued for any reason, the total liability is yours.

Business Names and Trademarks

As you establish and build your business, growth and success will make it increasingly valuable, and the symbol of that success will be your business name. Most things of value are worthy of protection, and as a means of protecting your business name, facilities exist to allow you to register that name. This registration will involve a fee of $109, and the registration is renewable every 3 years. There may also be a $14 search fee involved in the cost of setting this up to ensure that the name you require is not already in use, or you may wish to search the business names website (www.search.asic.gov.au/gns001.html). If you're operating under your own name you don't need to register that name, but the name you do register cannot be similar to someone else's name, it cannot be misleading, offensive or otherwise unsuitable. Once the business name registration certificate has been received, it must be clearly displayed near the entrance of the business.

Registering your business name will give you a certain level of protection but it's by no means totally protected. For a higher level of protection, you may want to consider registering your business name as a trademark. This involves making application to IP Australia via an application form at the cost of $150, and if this application is successful, one then needs to pay a $300 registration fee. This fee is renewable every 10 years and so it may be more cost effective than the simple registration of a business name. To find out more about this, and to scan the current trademarks to ensure that the one you wish to use is available, contact IP Australia directly or go to their website, www.ipaustralia.gov.au

Records and Record Keeping
As a primary contact healthcare practitioner it's in your interests to keep clear, concise and current records relating to clients, staff, tax, GST, insurance, legal and financial issues. This is particularly relevant in the area or client files and case notes. The quality of these documents often forms the focus of malpractice and negligence law suits, and the necessity for rigour in this are should never be underestimated.

Client interview forms will be discussed in more detail later, but as a general rule, client files should contain:
- The clients name and contact details
- Date of birth
- Healthcare provider
- Nationality
- Marital status
- Details regarding children
- The clients normal medical adviser
- Medication history
- Medical history
- Information regarding allergies or sensitivities to medications or any other substances
- The date of the consultation
- The reasons for the consultation
- Clinical findings from the consultation
- Medications prescribed or services provided
- Treatment plan and proposed outcomes
- Written copies of any advice that may be given, including referrals for other investigations or services.

The notes related to subsequent consultations should include the date of consultation, the results of the original treatment and any subjective comments by the client regarding the treatment (in their own words), any further treatment or advice, as well as written copies of referrals for any further investigations or services. These notes should avoid the use of jargon or abbreviations, they should not contain alterations to the notes or additional notes written into margins. Any additions or alterations to these notes that have to be made should be signed and dated by the practitioner. The comments made should be objective and avoid making any unsubstantiated conclusions or opinions. If handwritten, the notes should be clear and legible. Client files and case notes should be stored securely, and accessible only by the receptionist and the practitioner.

Insurance
All of the stock and equipment, fixtures, fittings and premises used in the operation of your business require some level of protection, as do you, your staff and your income. Insurance policies are the normal method of providing this protection and vast numbers of insurance providers and polices exist to assist you in this process. Following are the main types of policies that should be considered.

Public Liability
This type of policy protects you against claims made for damages by a person who may have injured themselves whilst on your premises. These policies will normally cover you up to a fixed dollar value, these commonly being one , five or ten million dollars, and the cost of the premiums will be relative to the extent of the cover.

Professional Indemnity
This type of policy protects you against claims for professional malpractice or negligence, so that your personal assets may not threatened by such claims. It may cover such things such as:
* Liability in the course of practice
* Nuisance claims
* Claims made against partners or employees
* Claims made under the Trade Practices or Fair Trading Acts

This type of policy may also provide cover for issues related to the teaching of students, or charges of liable or slander. There's normally a defined maximum level of one, five or ten million dollars, for example, and the cost of the premiums will be relative to the level of cover. There are several large insurance companies that provide these types of policies, and one of the main companies offering these policies is Marsh, whose contact details can be found in the White Pages telephone directory for most capital cities around Australia. Your professional association can usually provide you with the details of insurers normally used by the professional members of the association. Significant discounts on premiums may be available to members of some professional associations, and professional indemnity insurance may be required for professional membership.

A point to be beware of in regard to this form of insurance is that in the event that you have a locum practicing in your clinic, if that person does not have their own professional indemnity insurance and a malpractice or negligence issue arises from their actions, you may be joined in a legal action against the locum.

Another point to take note of here is that the policy may not protect you if at the time of the event in question:
- You are inebriated.
- You've been found to be using products or procedures that cannot be supported scientifically or by a panel of your peers.
- You've been acting dishonestly.

There are a number of different types of professional indemnity insurance policies, the main one being "occurrence coverage", where you're covered against incidents that may arise from a year when the policy was active. This policy protects the policy holder against claims made during the time that the insurance was in place, but where the claim is made at a time after the policy has expired. Another type of professional indemnity policy is the "claims made" variety, where coverage only exists while the policy is active.

Because of the importance of these policies, it may be wise to seek legal advice as a means of interpreting the policy and having its implications and limitations clearly defined as issues such as retirement, or a change of the business structure may affect the status of the insurance coverage. It's useful to be aware that the legal advisor may have to be briefed on the unique aspects of your method of practice to be able to competently advise you on the policy.

Income Protection
This type of policy insures you against loss of income due to various unforeseen circumstances. It generally provides for a fixed amount for a fixed period of time.

Clinic Contents
This form of insurance covers the policy holder against theft, or by other means, loss of the contents of the clinic. It's important to be aware here that some policies will only provide the replacement value of the item or items in question. A policy providing new rather than replacement value should be sought. To expedite claims that may be made on the policy, one should maintain an asset register, listing details such as:

- The cost of each item in the clinic.
- When the item was purchased.
- Who the item was purchased from.
- Details regarding the items depreciation schedule and lease details if leased.
- If sold, the date the item was sold, who purchased it and for what price.

This asset register must be properly maintained and a copy of the held off-site.

Dispensary Contents

These may or may not be covered under the clinic contents policy, but due to the nature of some dispensaries (because of size or diversity etc) , it may be required to be covered under a separate policy. Once again, it's wise to be covered for the new rather than replacement value of the dispensary stock, and it's essential that accurate and current stock records be maintained and copies of these records held off-site, to allow accurate claims on this policy to be made.

Fire

Insurance against damage by fire may form part of other policies, but it's important to be aware that the improper storage of flammable or hazardous materials, building alterations, improperly installed electrical appliances and old or faulty electrical wiring, may affect the success of claims made on these types of policies.

Burglary

As with fire insurance, insurance against burglary may form part of other policies, but claims made on this policy may be affected by the type and number of window and door locks about the premises, and any other issues that may have an impact on the ability of an intruder to gain entry onto the premises.

Cash on Hand

This covers theft and other means by which cash on the premises may be lost, and as with burglary insurance, the general level of clinic security may have some bearing on the ability to make claims on this policy.

Cash in Transit

This type of policy insures against the loss of cash being transported to banks etc.

Glass

Whilst insurance against the cost of breakage of glass in windows etc may seem as if it should be covered in a general policy, it is often not and a separate policy may have to be generated to cover this possibility.

Key Person
Policies are available to cover the losses that may be incurred by the business if a person upon whom the business is reliant, a receptionist for example, falls ill or is otherwise unable to attend the clinic for an extended period of time.

Product Liability
This policy indemnifies the policy holder against any issues that may arise by the use of therapeutic products produced by the practitioner or the clinic.

Partnership Insurance
This type of policy may protect the policy holder against the actions of one or more partners involved in the business.

Miscellaneous Issues
Law of Contract
You should be aware that what you can and cannot do as a practitioner may be determined in accordance with the law that relates to contracts. A contract comes about when you agree to treat a person who is seeking help for a particular ailment. Once you make an appointment for a client, you have established the basis for a contract and there is expectation on both sides that the requirements of the contract are fulfilled. If those requirements are not fulfilled, a breach of the contract may have occurred, and legal remedies exist to provide satisfaction to the aggrieved party.

The contract may be verbal or may be put into writing, and may not be binding without payment, either full or in part. It's important to understand here that for the purposes of a malpractice or negligence claim, payment or the lack of it may not affect the outcome of the claim if the claim is based on a breach of contract.

Consent to Treatment
Treatment without consent may constitute assault and battery. In regard to the consent itself, that consent needs to be informed, that is, the client needs to be fully aware of what they're consenting to. A case for negligence may be raised if a practitioner fails to provide the client with sufficient information about products or procedures related to the treatment, and the potential risks or dangers inherent in the provision of services or use of products. Consent may not be required in an emergency where any delay in treatment could endanger the person's life.

Consent itself may be written, oral or is more frequently implied via body language that communicates acceptance of a procedure such as the extension of an arm for the purposes of taking a pulse reading or determining blood pressure.

Consent must be made voluntarily, and be made by a client who is over 16 years of age, sane, sober and conscious, and consent must cover the procedure actually performed. Further consent must be sought for any new procedure that is about to be performed, and if any of these conditions are not present, it may be deemed that consent has not been given.

Telephone Consultations

There may be times when, because a client is unable to travel to the clinic, an interview needs to be conducted by phone. This is perfectly feasible as long as the following issues are kept in mind:

- The consultation should be in the nature of a follow-up only. The client should have already been examined by someone competent and qualified to carry out an initial examination and the practitioner conducting the telephone interview is in possession of, or has sighted, any relevant documentation that has been generated as a result of the initial examination.
- The clients progress should be competently evaluated.
- Receipts for such services should clearly identify that the consultation was done by telephone.

Both parties should be aware that healthcare insurance rebates may not be able to be claimed on this form of consultation.

Importing Medicines

From time to time, one may wish to prescribe medicines that are available for use overseas, but for various reasons, are unapproved for supply in Australia. Those wishing to import medicines that are unapproved should be aware that it may be possible to import them for personal use by the importer or their immediate family, but it is illegal to import and then use these products for commercial purposes.

Business Licences

Before one is able to operate a healthcare practice, various approvals need to be granted by a significant number of government departments and regulatory authorities, particularly if one employs staff. Some of these agencies have already been mentioned, but it may be prudent to ensure that one has fully met one's obligations in this area by contacting the Business Licences Information Service, as it's known in NSW and Tasmania, or its equivalent in other states (see details in the Resources section).

4. Taxation
Goods and Services Tax (GST)
The goods and services tax was introduced in July 2000 as a means of shifting the tax burden from indirect, to direct taxation. As a tax on the purchase of goods and services, it is generally applied in most areas at a rate of 10%, with some exceptions that apply to the healthcare industry. The services of most mainstream healthcare practitioners apart from homoeopaths, masseurs and nutrition consultants do not attract GST. The GST exempt status for providers of natural therapies is subject to review in June 2003, and may be subject to some form of registration for the profession. The application of GST on applicable therapeutic goods and services is not mandatory if the clinics annual turnover is below $50,000.

Whilst the services of some providers may not attract GST, the medicines, depending on what they are, who prescribes them and how they're used, may. Medicines prescribed by medical practitioners that are available through the Pharmaceutical Benefits Scheme, and medicines prescribed by chiropractors, osteopaths and acupuncturists do not attract GST, and the price of folic acid supplements does not attract GST. However, medicines prescribed by naturopaths and herbalists will attract GST unless they're fully consumed at the time of the consultation.

The GST charged on goods and services supplied to clients must be paid to the Australian Taxation Office (ATO). The GST component of the price paid for goods and services that are purchased as a part of normal clinic business activity can be retrieved from the ATO in the form of tax credits. For this and many other reasons it's imperative that you keep all relevant receipts and paperwork that pertain to commercial transactions, and ensure that all receipts are valid tax receipts, listing the GST component, the ABN of the business that supplied the receipt (discussed later) and headed with the words, "Tax Invoice". The GST amounts are lodged with the ATO every three months along with the regular income taxation payments discussed below.

You need to register with the ATO to become part of the GST system, but prior to doing this you need to acquire an ABN, because your ABN becomes your GST registration number.

Registration, Business Numbers and Other Requirements
When you commence business, you become a new tax payer, and as such you must register your business with the ATO and acquire a separate tax file number for it. The tax file number may also be required if you want to open a bank account on behalf of the business.

Unless your annual turnover is below $50,000 per year, you'll also need to acquire an ABN. This is a system used by the ATO to assist in the regulation and monitoring of commercial activity. If you don't acquire an ABN, any other business making payments to you that are in excess of $50, must withhold 48% of those payments and transfer those amounts to the ATO (you can retrieve the balance when you lodge your tax). For this reason, even if your annual income is less that $50,000 and you elect not to acquire an ABN, the increased paperwork involved and the reduced cash flow that stems from this decision may make it unwise not to get an ABN.

The forms related to registration and application are available from the ATO and may also be available from post offices and the ATO website.

Income Tax
Taxation is calculated as a percentage of income, after various allowable deductions have been subtracted from the gross income, and it is paid to the ATO. This percentage varies in accordance with the level of income, and the nature of the entity that has generated the income, but it may be anywhere from 0 to around 49%.

The percentage of tax payable and the means by which it's paid varies with who or what attracts the tax liability. For the purposes of this chapter, the focus will be on business related tax, rather than personal tax.

The means of paying tax is through the Business Activity Statement (BAS). For healthcare practitioners, the BAS is lodged with the ATO every 3 months, on or before the 21st day of the month following the end of the tax period, these ending on October, February, April and July. Along with this you need to pay GST and lodge your GST credits, as well as the appropriate tax for any person in your employ. If you operate a business a BAS must be lodged regardless of your level of income. The appropriate forms for handling these matters can be sourced from the ATO, or newsagents, or they can be filled out on interactive forms through the ATO website. The ATO currently make CDs available that contain information that relate to all of these issues, as well as CDs that can assist with record keeping. The ATO may also make field officers available to personally advise business operators on all of these issues.

Tax Deductions

The expenses incurred in operating a business can be deducted from the businesses gross income, thereby reducing the taxable income and therefore the tax liability. The cost of the following items may be deducted from taxable income:

- Costs related to the business premises
  - Lease or rental payments
  - Rates
  - Power
  - Telephone
- Costs related to plant and equipment
  - Depreciation can be claimed on the purchase price of major items
  - Running costs can be claimed
  - Depending on the type of item, lower cost items may be fully deductible- your accountant can advise on this
  - Hire or lease payments
- Stock purchases
- Purchase of tools such as stethoscopes, examination couches etc (note that the first set of tools you buy may be subject to depreciation rather than direct deduction- see below)
- Office costs- Business stationery
- Subscriptions
- Association fees
- Purchase cost of professional journals and newsletters
- Advertising costs
- Yellow Pages advertising
- Business cards
- Pamphlets
- Television or radio advertising
- Employee expenses
- Salary and wages
- WorkCover
- Superannuation
- Payroll or other taxes
- Any other compensation paid to an employee
- Registered tax agent fees
- Tax advice given by lawyers
- Insurance
  - Building
  - Equipment
  - Sickness and accident etc
- Key person (note that the ATO may make any payments from such a policy taxable if you claim the premiums as a deduction)

- Superannuation (note that with personal superannuation, the first $3000 invested is fully tax deductible, after which it's 75% is deductible up to specific age related contribution limits.
- Interest on borrowed money where money has been used in the business to generate an income
- Motor vehicle expenses- the costs of using a vehicle for legitimate commercial activity can be used as a tax deduction. There are 2 popular methods of calculating this deduction.
  - Use a logbook for a minimum of 3 months. Note must be taken of where the activity took place, the nature and date of the activity and distance covered, the speedometer reading at the end of each of these trips, and the make and model as well as the engine capacity and registration number of vehicle. The total business distance travelled is then calculated as a percentage of the total distance travelled by the vehicle and the percentage of business use is applied to the total running cost of the vehicle, including registration, repairs, tyres, fuel, oil and so on, and the percentage running cost figure used as the vehicle expense deduction.
  - The second method of calculating this deduction is via the rate per kilometre method. Again, a log book is used to record the vehicles details and the travel details, and the deduction is based on a fixed rate per kilometre of business related distance travelled. This rate varies with the engine size of the vehicle. It should be noted that you cannot make a deduction claim for travel from home to your place of business or back again.
- Business related travel- This may be local or overseas travel related to business. Claims may be made for the cost of air, bus, train, or tram travel, taxis, car hire, meals, accommodation and incidentals if travelling out of town.
- Repairs- This is applicable to repairs to buildings, property, equipment or anything else used in the business to generate an income. The value of any improvements made to these items should be added to the total value of the item for the purposes of depreciation.
- Home office expenses- These expenses apply to a home office or home clinic, which is defined by the ATO as a separate space from the rest of the dwelling. This space should not be accessible from the rest of the dwelling either by interconnecting doors or staircases and there should be a fixed and permanent barrier that separates this space from the rest of the dwelling. Claims may be made as a percentage of floor space used. Therefore, if the home office or clinic occupies one tenth of the total floor space of the dwelling, tax deduction claims may be made on one tenth of the rent, mortgage interest, insurance, council rates, utilities, telephone and other expenses (not telephone installation costs). The ATO may apply a limit to the amount of the deductions here. Note that if you have a home business and you sell your home, the sale price may attract capital gains tax.

- Office plant and equipment- depreciation may be claimed for these items when used solely for business purposes. They may include things such as curtains, carpets, light fittings, computers, printers, professional library, and shelves. A comprehensive list of items for which depreciation may be claimed should be obtained from the ATO. See below for a brief discussion on depreciation.

Deductions cannot be claimed on the cost of capital expenditure items such as buildings (i.e. the purchase price), business names, copyrights, patents, fees or charges incurred in establishing a new business, company formation expenses, or the cost of purchasing a business (see the ATO for a comprehensive list of these items). These are things that provide the business with a long term benefit and therefore cannot be claimed as deductions.

Depreciation
Because the value of some items, particularly those with a high purchase price, may reduce over time, claims may be made for this loss of value in accordance with the ATO schedules of depreciation. Depreciation schedules are calculated in two ways. Firstly on the basis that the item in question has a fixed useable life, say five years, and that every year that item would lose 20% of its value. In this case the depreciable rate would be 20% of the items original cost per year. This method of calculation is called prime cost.

The second method, referred to as diminishing value, uses a higher percentage rate and the dollar amount claimed in the first year is subtracted from the original purchase price. For example, an item with a purchase price of $1000 might be assigned an annual depreciation rate of 15%. In the first year, at the 15% rate, the claimable depreciation would be $150, leaving an un-depreciated or written down value of $850 at the end of that year. In the second year, the 15% rate applied to the new value of $850 would allow for a depreciation claim of $127.50, and so on, until the written down value dropped to zero. If one disposes of an asset, the difference between the sale proceeds and the written down or residual value of the item at the time of the disposal may be taxable, and the rest of the residual value may be claimed as a tax deduction. Depreciation rates or scales for particular items may be obtained from the ATO.

Miscellaneous Issues
It may be prudent to calculate your tax before you pay it to the ATO and deposit it into a separate bank account every week, to ensure that you're never without sufficient funds to cover your tax liability.

As mentioned earlier, it's critical that receipts for every transaction and every item are kept, in the event that the ATO carry out an audit on your business and you're asked to provide evidence of claims.

For more information on this subject contact the ATO, and please note that the information on taxation is given as a guide only, and is not designed to replace the advice of a qualified financial adviser, tax agent or the ATO.

5. Safety and Hygiene
Occupational Health and Safety Requirements
Occupational health and safety guidelines are just that- guidelines, rather than laws. These guidelines have been put into place to protect staff, clients and the community. If one were shown to be negligent in any of the areas covered by these guidelines, it may be seen that you have failed in your duty of care and you may be held to be liable for any damages that might arise from resultant legal actions.

These guidelines as they relate to healthcare clinics mean that you are required to ensure that your premises and practices are clean, safe and properly maintained. The guidelines include the following issues:
- Any needles used should be new or if not should be properly sterilised and any skin penetration that occurs as part of the practice should be done in accordance with accepted sterility guidelines and the Skin Penetration Act.
- Any food or drink supplied to clients or staff on the premises must be supplied in accordance with the local food and drink preparation safety regulations.
- All walkways and passageways should be kept free of obstructions, and all walking surfaces should be free from materials that may cause clients to slip or fall.
- Toilets and any other facilities that are provided should be clean and properly maintained.
- Emergency exits should be kept clear.
- Approved smoke alarms should be fitted in the approved manner (the local fire brigade can advise on this)
- Examination or bodywork couches should be properly maintained and one should ensure that infirm or elderly clients can climb upon them and get off them again with ease.
- All other equipment that exists within the practice should be properly maintained and have the minimal potential to cause harm.

If you're not sure about anything else in this area, walk around your practice and look for anything that may have even the remotest possibility of causing problems for clients or staff and fix it. You should also guard against the transmission of infectious agents such as viruses, bacteria and other micro-organisms from one client to the next, or the contamination of wounds, using the appropriate barrier techniques and sterility procedures. Avoid direct or unguarded contact with wounds and wash well before and after physical contact with all clients. In addition, all staff should be aware of the procedures that need to be followed in the case of a fire or other emergency, and the relevant evacuation procedures, and the practitioner in attendance should be properly trained in current first aid measures.

Good occupational health and safety practices can help to promote a professional practice appearance, help you to avoid costly litigation, and will help to avoid possible claims made on your public liability insurance.

6. Ethics and Negligence
Core Ethics Issues
One needs to tread very carefully in this area. Laws and their application by courts are based, for the most part, on ethics and ethical considerations. Therefore, to ignore ethics and their implications is at worst to invite claims for negligence or face prosecution under criminal law, and at best to cause distress to clients or the community.

The are a number of major ethical issues that relate to the provision of healthcare.
- Always be honest in your dealing with clients, staff and all of those with whom you interact. Your marketing activities should be based on honesty, the statements you make and impressions you give must be honest and open and comply with all of the relevant laws, regulations and statutes.
- Scrupulously avoid anything that may cause others to see you as something which you are not qualified or entitled to be. Any action, appearance or statement that may cause others to assume that you are a medical doctor, chiropractor, osteopath, physiotherapist, naturopath, acupuncturist, veterinarian, dentist or other professional person where you hold neither the qualification or entitlement to do so is unethical.
- All communications between the practitioner and the client should be clearly understood by both parties. Given the numerous languages and cultures that abound within our society, it's incumbent upon us to ensure that all communication is clear.
- Any risks that may be inherent in the use of certain medicines, procedures or practices should be clearly and comprehensively conveyed to the client. Few methods and materials are without some risk, even if the resultant problem is only mild and transitory.

- The development of a sexual relationship with a client is one of the most serious breaches of professional ethics and yet one of the most common. It involves a breach of trust, violates the role of the therapist, it exploits the vulnerability of the client, and is not validated by consent. Should a consensual relationship appear to be imminent, carefully consider the ramifications but immediately cease acting as the other party's practitioner. The intimacy associated with the sharing of information can be a source of potential problems for both sides but this sharing of information should never be misconstrued as anything other than what is necessary for the client/practitioner relationship to function properly.

- The reasons for every action that is performed on a client, and every lifestyle modification, medicine prescribed and treatment protocol recommended should be clearly and simply explained to the client.

- All costs involved in the treatment, and the time required to perform that treatment should be clearly and simply explained to the client at the outset of the appointment, preferably at the time of booking the appointment. This saves unnecessary confusion and a potential lack of trust by the client.

- Any written or verbal transactions, client records, reports and all other matters pertaining to the treatment of a client must be held in strict confidence. Issues related to client confidentiality form a frequent subject for legal discussion. The client should be able to expect that information that they give will be kept confidential- this expectation must be upheld. In most states, access to the complete client records by the client is given at the discretion of the practitioner. Whilst clients themselves have no natural legal right to their records in most states, they can and should have access to a summary of these records if they request them, and they have the rights of ownership of all laboratory and radiology reports. Client records may be subpoenaed by a court or become the subject of a court order, or may be released if the records reveal a serious and identifiable risk to the client, a third party or the community. In Victoria, under the Health Records Act, passed in 2001, Victorians do have a legal right to these records. For more on this see www.health.vic.gov.au/hsc .

- Client information should only be transmitted with the express permission of the client. For these reasons it's wise to avoid recording anything other than the facts. Anything that you note that may be of a subjective nature, that may convey conclusions or cause any distress or embarrassment to the client should be avoided.

- Special note should be taken of the dynamics of the client/practitioner relationship and the effect that they may have on the client. The disparity between the perceived power of the client and the practitioner in this relationship can have a profound effect on the quality and impact of communication by the practitioner to the client. By virtue of his or her training, experience and credentials, the practitioner is in a position of dominance. What may appear to the practitioner to be a passing comment of little import may be seen by the client to have major significance. Verbal or non-verbal cues may be magnified manifold and the client may be fearful of the practitioner making some dire discovery regarding their health. All of these things and more highlight the need to act in a caring and professional manner and be aware of the ways in which communications may be received by the client. The disempowerment of the client within the confines of the client practitioner relationship can be partially addressed by getting the person actively involved in the planning of their own recovery process and ensuring that as fully as is possible, they know exactly why they're being asked to do certain things and what the likely outcomes of those actions will be.

- One should take an ethical and responsible approach to one's skills and knowledge base, and for this reason it's wise to keep abreast of any technical, legal or other developments that relate to your profession and practice.
- It is unethical to criticise other members of the healing professions. It brings one's own profession into disrepute and may lead to legal action by the aggrieved person or group to which he or she belongs. If you have concerns over the actions of any other member of the profession, it's appropriate to seek the advice of your own professional association as to the best course of action.
- You should strive to maintain a safe and hygienic practice and ensure that you maintain all appropriate insurance policies.
- You should do nothing with staff or clients that may be seen as discriminatory on the basis of sex, race, disability, age or association (this latter referring to their association with political, social or any other groups).
- You should ensure that you're fit to practice. If you have an infectious disease you should either seek to have a locum replace you for the period during which the disease is potentially contagious or take the appropriate steps to ensure that the infection cannot be transmitted. You should also be mentally fit to practice, and should not be inebriated or in any other way unfit to meet the needs of your clients.

Client Appointments
Always allow enough time to effectively and professionally meet the needs of a client, although don't assume that more time produces better results. Time is rarely commensurate with the quality of the outcome and it tends to be what one does that has a greater influence on the results than how long one does it. Always endeavor to be punctual- an extra 20 minutes spent with the first client of the day penalises all of the clients that follow for that day, unless you make up the time somewhere else. Keep a clock within view and ensure that you start on time and finish on time. It's also appropriate to phone clients the day before their appointment to remind them of the event. This minimises the possibility of the client forgetting the appointment and minimises the possibility of mistakes being made in the client booking register such as clients being double booked.

The Business of Healing

Rebates

Many non-medical health services are rebatable through the various healthcare insurers that operate throughout Australia. In many circumstances, one needs to apply to the health insurance company via an application form before provider status can be acquired. It's appropriate that you keep up to date with which healthcare insurers will provide rebates for your services, and ensure that you have current lists of their service item numbers. These lists should be kept in the reception area to facilitate the production of proper receipts and to enable the receptionist to answer queries regarding rebates.

One should also be aware of the annual limits applied to the amount of rebate for particular services and the amount of rebate available per service. These amounts will vary between the various healthcare insurance companies. For example, IOR have an annual limit of $360 per person for chiropractic, naturopathic, acupuncture or homoeopathic services with 70% of the cost of the service (standard fee) covered by the insurance. IOR may also cover some of the costs of vitamins or supplements- many other funds do not provide this service. Grand United has an annual limit of $700 per person for chiropractic and $35 of the initial consultation, has an annual limit of $500 for naturopathy, acupuncture and homoeopathy, and cover $25 of the initial consultation. Grand United may also cover some of the costs of vitamins or supplements.

There have been numerous attempts over the years by some healthcare providers and others to falsify rebate claims for the purpose of financial gain- this is obviously unethical and illegal. There are several methods commonly employed and these are well known to the insurance industry which constantly monitors claims for these types of issues. They consist of things such as:
* Filling out a receipt for two items when only one has been performed, thus enabling the client to increase the value of the claim.
* Issuing receipts to family members or friends where the services claimed have not been provided.
* Receipts are issued and claims made for family members of the person for whom the services were provided, enabling the client to collect the rebate through the family member where the annual rebate limit has already been reached.
* Unqualified assistants performing services that would have been rebatable had they been performed by the qualified practitioner, but not if performed by the assistant.

Should a practitioner be discovered conducting any such fraudulent activities, they will generally be subject to expulsion from their professional association, have their service provider status with the health insurers cancelled and may be charged with criminal conduct.

Miscellaneous Issues
One is ethically and legally bound to provide a client with a refund if the product they've purchased is defective, or a product or service doesn't do what it was claimed that it could or would do.

Claims or statements should not be made that create unrealistic expectations by the client, nor should claims or statements be made that cannot be supported by acceptable evidence. For residents of NSW, those who make claims for products or services that cannot be supported scientifically may be subject to fines of up to $22,000.

It's useful to be aware that of the many acts and statutes that govern our actions as practitioners, we're also subject to criminal and civil law as well as consumer legislation. One should be aware of the provisions under the Trade Practices Act and Fair Trading legislation for misleading or deceptive behaviour. These Acts make it an offence to make claims for miracle cures etc, or to make false or misleading claims regarding one's level of experience or and qualifications, or make any other false representations about therapeutic goods or services.

If employing staff, it should be kept in mind that under a legal rule called Vicarious Liability, the employer is normally responsible for any damages that arise from the acts of an employee, and any problems that they may cause with clients or anyone else that they deal with on behalf of their employer.

Malpractice and Negligence
One of the most terrifying things that can happen to a healthcare practitioner is the threat of legal action for malpractice or negligence. As a means of preventing such things from occurring, various organisations and individuals have been able to identify specific groups of typical litigants- individuals who have a higher than normal propensity to raise malpractice or negligence claims against practitioners, in the hope that these individuals can more easily be recognised and the appropriate actions taken. Whilst caution should be exercised when dealing with these people, they should not be denied help simply because of their potential for complaints and litigation. Typical litigant categories include:

The Bargain Hunter- this person goes from practitioner to practitioner trying to get the best deal and the lowest price. He or she usually complains about the level of your fees and simply considers the healing process as a commercial transaction. It can be difficult to meet this person's expectations because of their inability to see past the dollars and cents issues. Failure to met their expectations can result in the client feeling dissatisfied to the point of becoming litigious. As a means of protecting yourself against any such complaints, it's wise to ensure that both of you understand each other and what your expectations of each other are. If necessary, draw up a contract outlining the responsibilities of each party, perhaps agreeing to a fixed number of appointments, after which the relationship may be terminated if one of the parties is unsatisfied with the outcomes. At the very least you should attempt to record the client's statements in their own words, as these may provide a useful basis of evidence should it be required at a later date.

The Devotee- thinks you are the most magnificent healer to have ever drawn breath and the results of your attentions will be nothing short of miraculous. It may be difficult to meet this person's expectations and failure to do so may lead to disappointment, and in severe cases, legal action to seek a remedy for these disappointing results. Once again, it's useful to ensure that both parties know exactly where each stands and that neither has illusions regarding your capacity to heal. It should be made very clear to the client who you are, what you are, what your capabilities and limitations are and what the likely treatment outcomes will be. Providing the client with written confirmation of these points and keeping a copy of this document can be valuable insurance against any legal action that may ensue from a relationship with such a person.

The Lawbreaker- may seek your help in defrauding medical insurers, employers and other potential sources of financial or material gain. They may also be seeking your assistance with the provision of certificates declaring them unfit for work. The obvious response here is to deny the request, determine what, if any, health needs the person may have, and treat these accordingly.

The Fragile Client- has a level of health which is so poor that almost anything may cause them to have a relapse into serious ill health, and the responsibility for the relapse may be assigned to you. With this client and all others you must be aware of your limitations and ensure that you don't extend yourself past them. Many of these clients may require referral to a practitioner with more experience in the area concerned. You should scrupulously avoid making claims that could imply that your competence, experience or qualifications allow you to deal with a situation with which you are unable to cope.

The Expert- takes a great deal of interest in all of the technical information, research and any other details surrounding his or her treatment. This person may make frequent requests for you to write all of these things down, and they may harbour a feeling that they know much more about what you do than you do yourself. They may complain that you're inept, and they may well use the technical details that you've supplied in writing to confirm this. With these and all other clients you should ensure that anything that you say or do can be substantiated, and you should be sure of your facts before launching into learned dissertations on the subject in question.

The Uncooperative Client- may expect you to heal them without their help and will blame you when they fail to get the expected results in the expected time. They may not accede to your requests for things such as x-rays or blood tests, and fail to follow through on your referral to other practitioners to assist in your treatment protocols. They may fail to keep appointments and ignore your recommendations. They are often dissatisfied with their progress, despite their failure to participate in their own healing and this dissatisfaction may give rise to legal action. It's useful to ensure that every instruction or request that you put to these individuals is made in writing as well as verbally, and you keep copies of all of these documents, and it's also useful to record the clients comments concerning these requests and instructions. At the outset you should be clear about what this type of client expects of you, and the client needs to be clear about what's expected of them. This is another situation that may benefit from the construction of a contract, copies of which should be signed and held by both parties, outlining the responsibilities of both parties, and giving expression to a fixed number of appointments over which the healing process should be carried out. The contract should also state that the failure of either party to meet their responsibilities may result in a termination of the relationship.

The Hypochondriac- may be seen to be imagining their ills, and these ills may or may not be real but should you miss finding and dealing with any of them, the unhappiness that arises may harden into legal action by the client. The best course of action here is to ensure that you're clear on exactly what the client wants you to treat, that both of you understand which issue is being dealt with, and agree to deal with only one thing at a time. Once again, this agreement may need to be committed to paper and copies held by both parties.

The Lonely Client- may be seeking services other than those for which you hold formal qualifications. Your qualifications, experience, the perception of power that may surround the healer and the interview process during which personal information may be shared, can all cause some clients to view the practitioner as a potential target for their physical or emotional affection, or outright sexual assault. Outside of having to repel a physical onslaught, the lonely clients misconceptions should be handled with care and sensitivity, and the therapeutic relationship reinforced. An overly forceful rejection of the clients affections may cause distress that not only damages the therapeutic relationship, but in extreme circumstances may give rise to negligence charges. Clients should always be dealt with in a professional and courteous manner that doesn't promise more than it should to effectively heal. Once again, you should know your limitations and if the therapeutic relationship cannot be maintained, the client should be referred to another practitioner.

The Emotionally Disturbed Client- may show signs of acute anxiety, may make unreasonable demands and have unreasonable expectations. If these things are apparent, one should not assume that every ache or pain is imagined. These things may well be real and the failure to properly deal with them may result in claims for damages arising from alleged negligence or malpractice. It's important to treat all claimed ailments as real unless proven to be otherwise, and scrupulously avoid overtly invalidating the clients view of reality. If possible the emotionally disturbed client should be given an appointment towards the end of the day to allow them more time if the consultation runs over the allotted period.

In all of these instances, it should be kept in mind that the greatest generator of complaints is a lack of rapport between the practitioner and the client. Breakdowns or failures in communication, and or a retaliatory attitude by the practitioner in the face of a complaint are probably the greatest reasons for complaints becoming legal actions. Any complaint you receive should be handled promptly, professionally and in a caring manner. Firstly, determine the basis of the clients complaint, what they would like done about it and when. We may assume that the client's intention is to see us gaoled and fined, when all they really require is an apology. If you receive any serious complaint or there is a threat of legal action, it would be wise to contact your association or malpractice insurer immediately. Try to resolve the issue with the complainant directly in a caring and calm manner, advise the other people in your practice of what's occurring, do not attempt to alter your records, and contact your legal advisers. On the issues of negotiation, contracts, and clients agreeing to follow treatment protocols, Getting to Yes, by Roger Fisher and William Ury, mentioned in the Suggested Texts section above, has some useful advice.

Malpractice or negligence complaints generally only find their way into a court where one or more of the following has occurred:
- Loss of life.
- Loss of health (mental or physical).
- Loss of income, future income or prospects.
- Nervous shock or stress.
- Where medical expenses have arisen as a result of the negligence.
- Where the service provided was unreasonable.
- Where a service was not provided and there was an expectation that it should have been.
- A service was provided that was unnecessary.
- Where access to reasonable records was denied.
- Where information about the clients condition was not provided.
- Where due care and skill were not exercised.
- Where there was a lack of respect for the clients needs, dignity or wishes.
- Where there was a failure to use a language that the client could understand.
- Where there was a failure to provide the client with a means of making an informed choice about healthcare options.
- Where there was a failure to provide the client with a prognosis.

For a case regarding malpractice or negligence to succeed you have to be shown to have:

- Disregarded your duty of care, for example failed to recognise a particular illness or failed to recommend a referral to someone who could- this can even be raised as an issue if you give someone advice on the street, at a party or anywhere else outside the clinic.
- Failed to warn of the potential side effects of a treatment.
- Failed to determine that the client had a history of reactions to therapeutic goods or services that you provide.
- Failed to ensure that the client will not have reactions to currently used drugs etc as a result of the prescription of your goods or services.
- Acted in a manner that failed to meet the requisite standard for that practice. This is determined by putting the same circumstances to one or more of one's peers, to see if they would have acted in the same way as that done by the person who is subject to the charges.
- Acted in a manner proscribed by your professional associations standards as unethical or negligent.
- Acted in a manner which is outside your area of expertise.
- Acted in a manner that cannot be substantiated by properly controlled human clinical studies or a recognised and refereed text or manual.
- Acted in a manner that falsely implied that you held specialist knowledge, training, experience or skills.
- Referred a client to another practitioner for diagnosis or treatment of a serious health problem and failed to follow up on the referral.

To win a court case against you the plaintiff (the person taking the action against you) must have one or more of these points upheld and the injury must be able to be compensated. It should also be noted that clinical inexperience is not a valid defence against a negligence or malpractice claim.

As a means of limiting the potential for litigation, apart from the points mentioned above, the following points may be of use:

- Use things such as client sign-in registers so that there's a record that the client did see you for treatment.
- Use written rather than verbal guidance or warnings if you've asked the client to see another practitioner for other treatment or diagnosis.
- Record details of client non-compliance, keep records up to date, legible and accurate, and keep records for at least seven years.
- To diminish potential accusations of tampering with client records, don't erase anything from records, don't squeeze in notes and fully record everything you do.
- Be aware that if, for the purposes of profit, you create the perception that you are a member of any other profession which you're unqualified to be, and

you fail in the duty of care normally expected of someone with these credentials, you may also be subject to prosecution.

- Be aware that you may create a similar perception if, as a non-medical practitioner, you appear to be undertaking medical diagnosis by the use of standard medical diagnostic tools such as stethoscopes, sphygmomanometers etc. State based regulations and the interpretation by individual states of the relevant federal laws differ somewhat from one state to the next. In Queensland for example, a very dim view is taken of non-medical healthcare providers using medical diagnostic tools.
- Ensure that in the case of a serious life threatening disease or one which you are unqualified or inexperienced to handle, unless you have medical or specialist qualifications, the client should be advised in writing that you are not assisting with this disease but their general health, this treatment is not medical treatment, and that they should maintain contact with their medical adviser.
- You should never advise a client to cease or modify the use of medicines or treatments prescribed by another practitioner without the consent of that practitioner.
- Unless you have the appropriate medical or specialist qualifications you should avoid making statements that could be conceived as being part of an attempt at diagnosis- doing this may infer that you are practicing medicine.
- Unless you are appropriately qualified you should also avoid claiming that you can treat or cure serious illness.
- Be aware that a negligence claim may be mounted if you refuse to treat someone on the basis that the person is abusive or unco-operative.
- Note also that failure to provide for the needs of your established clientele in the event that you retire, go away on vacation or change your address, and the client experiences a severe medical problem, may result in legal action. Always give reasonable notice if you intend to terminate the therapeutic relationship for whatever reason in writing, refer to the client to another practitioner, and always allow the client some means of contacting you if you're away.
- A malpractice claim may be raised against you if a client is touched without their expressed (verbally or in writing) or implied (via body language etc) permission. This action may be taken through the use of a law referred to as "trespass to the person".

Finally on this issue, consent to treatment is another area that can be associated with malpractice or negligence actions. For consent to be legally capable of being given, the client must be over sixteen years of age, otherwise consent must be sought from a parent or guardian. Consent must be given knowingly, therefore the person must be if full possession of their faculties, they should be capable of understanding what they are consenting to and able to understand English or whichever language is used by the practitioner.

Miscellaneous Issues
In the event that a practitioner is found guilty of malpractice or negligence, the penalties may range from a reprimand, to orders for counselling, suspension, de-registration, or fines. In most states of Australia, negligence or malpractice actions must be commenced within six years of the event concerned. In Queensland the time limit for this action is three years.

A number of defences may be mounted to negligence or malpractice claims, and generally, the defence used will relate specifically to the allegations that have been made. Among these may be that the client had full knowledge of the risks involved, and voluntarily took on that risk, or that the client contributed fully or in part to the problem

Parties other than the practitioner may be drawn into a negligence or malpractice claim. These may be the employer of the practitioner and the manufacturer of any therapeutic goods or equipment involved in the claim. The claim may be made by the client, their parent or guardian or other person on behalf of the client, or a health service provider.

For more information on the legal processes associated with negligence or malpractice cases see Chapter 8 of Complementary Medicine: Ethics and Law, by Michael Weir.

7. Practice Design, Location and Practice Options
Each different form of business has its' own idiosyncrasies related to what it does, and where and how it does it, and non-medical healthcare clinics are no exception. The layout and design of the business needs to take these idiosyncrasies into consideration if one aims to maximise the potential of the business.

Clinic Layout and Design
Healthcare clinics put certain demands upon the spaces that they occupy. Most of these demands relate to the primary aim of the practice- client wellness, with consideration being given to the often somewhat secondary aims of profitability and staff wellbeing. These are the main drivers for the layout of an efficient and effective clinic. Of major importance in all of the areas that relate to the layout of the clinic is something that should dovetail neatly with marketing- style.

The colours used, furniture selected, and the shapes and textures of all of the objects used in the clinic as well as the way that they're arranged should all reflect a consistency in style that supports what you want your business to say about you. A clinic specialising in the meeting the needs of the upper levels of the socio-economic strata will not be well served by selecting second hand government furniture and presenting rooms painted in mismatched pastel shades. Similarly, the clients of a clinic in a working class area will not necessarily identify well with a practice painted in stark colours and furnished with objects made in Sweden from leather, glass and stainless steel.

Colours can have a significant impact on the clinical outcomes achieved by the practice. A number of good texts are available on the subject of colour therapy. Let There Be Light by Darius Dinshah, The Power of Color by Morton Walker and The Healing Power of Colour-zone Therapy by Joseph Corvo are some of the better ones. Colour therapy has a fairly interesting history. First described in 1810 by Johann Wolfgang Von Goethe in his book Zur Farbenlehre (Theory of Colours), Goethe outlined the psychological effects of colour. This body of work was added to in 1878 by Edwin Babbitt in his book, Principles of Light and Color. Spending some time researching this subject can provide significant benefits and can add greatly to the ability of the clinic itself to assist in the healing process.

Careful consideration needs to be given to the messages communicated by the style that one imposes on one's surroundings, and the selection of the correct style can make the clinic an enormously powerful marketing tool.

The clinic itself consists of several key elements.

The Entrance
The entrance-way and front door should look clean, professional and welcoming. The entrance-way should be free of anything that may obstruct the entrance or cause anyone using the entrance to stumble, and it should be free from surfaces that may be slippery when wet.

The door should carry the name of the clinic, the name of the practitioners, the clinic logo, street address, hours of operation telephone number and after-hours telephone number (normally a mobile phone used by the principal practitioner). An "open" and "closed" sign (one that doesn't flap and rattle when the door is used) can also be useful to let potential clients know whether or not the business is operating.

If funds allow, an air lock (consisting of 2 doors separated by a short passageway) provides an excellent means of reducing street noise, and minimising air-conditioning expense if air-conditioners are used, as an air-lock diminishes the amount of conditioned air escaping from the clinic when the door is opened. Avoid stairs if at all possible as many clients may have difficulty walking, and it's also useful to ensure that anyone in a wheelchair can gain access to the clinic without difficulty. The door itself should be able to be opened with a minimum of exertion.

The Business of Healing

Reception/Waiting Area
This should be immediately inside the front door, and if possible, one should avoid situating the waiting room outside a consulting room, as the clients privacy may be compromised by the proximity to the waiting area. Verandahs with views towards parks, gardens or other peaceful outdoor scenes can help to promote relaxation for clients awaiting the consultation. There should be sufficient chairs in the waiting room to cope with clients and anyone accompanying them (the minimum number of chairs should be five). The chairs themselves should be comfortable, properly designed (this is especially important in a clinic specialising bodywork, chiropractic or osteopathy) and of a style that's consistent with the image one intends to promote. The chairs should be facing the reception desk rather than each other, as forcing the people using them to face each other across the waiting room can create discomfort.

The colours chosen for the reception area should be consistent with the colours used in your marketing tools (signage, business cards, brochures etc), and they should be soothing and hopefully unique.

There should be a table, or combination table and magazine rack situated within easy reach of the chairs, for the purpose of carrying brochures promoting the activities of the clinic and other related businesses that refer clients to you (you should regularly check that this generosity is being reciprocated), and magazines that may be of interest to your clients and anyone who comes with them. The magazines that you choose should be current, and selected to promote or enhance your image, whilst not straying too far from what the typical inhabitants of the waiting area would normally read if given the choice.

For the small amount of cost involved (approximately $160 per year for rental and $6 per 15L bottle of pure water) a water fountain in the reception/waiting area is an excellent investment. You may or may not wish to have music playing in this area, if so the music should be unique but unobtrusive, soothing without being soporific, and it should be remembered that there are fees payable for doing this. It's useful to devote one area of this space to children, and stock it with sturdy, non-toxic toys or games. An area where children can play prior to seeing the practitioner, or whilst their accompanying adults are attending the consultation, can be helpful in promoting harmony for everyone in the clinic.

The point of central focus in this space should be the reception desk. Careful thought needs to devoted to the design of this object because it's the key feature for anyone coming into the clinic and those who are spending time waiting to see the practitioner. Once again, the shape, texture and colour should be consistent with the image promoted by the clinic. Curved desks made from natural materials often communicate a more caring and thoughtful attitude than something consisting of straight lines, corners and synthetic materials. Mention should be made on or near the reception desk of the services provided, schedule of fees (this reduces confusion and promotes payment), and the healthcare insurers who rebate the services provided by the practice.

For the purposes of image promotion it can be useful to have the clinic logo featured prominently on or behind the reception desk, and some practitioners have made good use of large reproductions of their own photographs set on the wall behind the reception desk. Fresh flowers on the reception desk can be very attractive, but try to avoid anything that's likely to aggravate allergies or sensitivities. Great use can be made of the reception desk as a means of selling a small number of high volume retail products and seasonal products for things such as hay fever. This is a significant revenue centre for many clinics, and may turn over several hundred dollars every week.

Some clinics have found advantages in employing video monitors showing brief presentations on issues related to the services provided by the clinic, or health problems that the clinic specialises in dealing with.

Consulting/Treatment Rooms
Consideration should be given to how many of these will be required. It's important to think about having adequate room for expansion rather than limiting the growth of the clinic by limiting the amount of space that can be used for consulting or treatment, which are the primary functions of the clinic. Ideally, these rooms should be situated on the southern side of the building- the side normally least affected by the heating effects of the afternoon sun. The western side is the worst for this as it may be up to 10 degrees hotter here than on the other side of the building. If you have no choice in this matter, consider using some method of shading the outside of the wall- painting the wall white and placing potted trees, a trellis, or shade-cloth in front of it.

Thought should also be given to the rooms themselves, the furniture placement within them, lighting, and the effects of these factors on the client. The room should be neat, tidy and uncluttered by anything other that what's regularly used in the course of practice and one of the most important issues in this room is the placement of desks and chairs. The prompt establishment of rapport with the client will have a major bearing on communication and the subsequent resolution of the issue being dealt with. The interposition of a desk between the practitioner and the client can act as a barrier and slow the establishment of this rapport, and has the added detriment of restricting the view of body language- for the client as well as the practitioner. It also emphasises the power disparity between the practitioner and the client. Much has been written on this subject, and the conventional wisdom indicates that communication is optimised by minimising the physical barriers between both parties. Therefore, having the practitioner and client on the same side of the desk, or having them separated by one corner of the desk, tends to provide the best results. For more on this issue see The Medical Interview by Ainslie Meares, mentioned in the Suggested Reading section above.

In regard to chairs, the practitioners' chair should be properly designed to deal with the rigours of regular use, and there should be 3 chairs to accommodate the client and others who may be accompanying them.

In relation to the orientation of furniture in relation to windows and doors, try to avoid having the client facing the sun through a window- this can cause distress to some clients, and leave your face in shadow, making it difficult to establish good communication. It's inadvisable for the practitioner to be situated between the client and the door, as this may convey the unconscious impression that the clients' means of escape are blocked. The clients' sense of freedom can also be diminished by orienting them with their back to a wall, and nor should they be put in a position facing the door where anyone entering through that door will distract them and break the visual communication between the practitioner and the client. Side-on to the door seems to provide the best results.

Colour and lighting can also influence the mental and emotional impact on the client. Oppressively low ceilings can be made to appear less so by painting the ceiling a lighter colour than the walls, and lighting direction can also influence the perceived height of the ceiling. Similarly, rooms where high ceilings may be a disadvantage can have this impression diminished by using lighter colours on walls and manipulating the direction of the lighting. Uncomfortably large rooms can be made to feel smaller by using large, darker items of furniture, and perceived room size can be increased by using smaller, lighter coloured objects of furniture. The use of landscape or jungle scenes in paintings or the installation of a window can also give the impression that the room is larger than what it actually is. The minimum ceiling height should be 9 feet.

The ability to lighten or darken the room is also useful (for Iridology/microscopy etc), and dimming the lights increases shadow which reduces the perceived size of the room, should it be an issue. The incoming light should be natural if at all possible, otherwise, if fluorescent lights are used they should be full spectrum. Normal (cool white) fluorescent lights may emit wavelengths that can raise blood cortisol and ACTH levels, diminish vitamin D production, increase vitamin A requirements, increase hyperactivity, reduce concentration, promote fatigue, increase irritability and alcohol craving, and increase melanoma and eye inflammation risk. The speed at which electricity cycles through fluorescent lights may also have an impact on diseases such as epilepsy.

Massage or examination tables, unless bodywork is the principle modality practiced in the room, should be moved against or close to a wall, such that the clients right side when lying prone (the area normally receiving the most attention in an abdominal examination) is facing the centre of the room. Their proximity to the wall when being examined can also reduce the potential for clients to feel exposed or vulnerable.

It's also important to ensure that consulting or treatment rooms are adequately ventilated. Normal respiration in a closed space increases the concentration of carbon dioxide within that space, which can increase fatigue and drowsiness, and can aggravate certain respiratory diseases. For these reasons, and because carbon dioxide is heavier than air and settles near to the floor, vents placed in the bottoms of doors can reduce the accumulation of this gas. Ventilation is also an important means of reducing the concentration of viruses that may be expelled by those suffering from viral respiratory diseases, and can reduce the possibility of mould growth.

The materials used to make the walls of the consulting or treatment rooms should minimise the transmission of noise and heat.

Lighting
Apart from the considerations mentioned above, if skylights are being installed, their benefits may be maximised and the costs minimised by ensuring that they emerge in the ceiling over walls or partitions, thereby illuminating more than just one room.

Floor Coverings
Hard wearing carpet is best in reception and consulting areas, and it's wise to check the carpets' dust rating and use the variety that generates a minimum of dust. Cork tiles are usually adequate for the dispensary- they're cheap to replace if anything is spilled on them and have the added bonus of allowing glass bottles to bounce rather than shatter on contact should one be dropped on them.

Dispensary
This area should be away from the heating effects of the western side of the building, it should be out of the reach of children, and it should be screened from the view of clients so that the focus is on the curative aspects of medicines rather than the mechanics of how they're made. It's useful to have a sink in this area, and allowance needs to be made for a minimum of 5 linear metres of shelving to carry the dispensary stock.

Change Room
For those specialising in bodywork, an ante-room off the consulting room gives clients a private and professional means of changing into a gown.

Kitchen
This is obviously useful as a space for staff to consume meals, and acts as a place where a cup of tea or some other refreshment can be made for clients or those accompanying them.

Laundry
An on-site laundry can be very useful where towels and gowns are regularly being washed.

Lecture Area
A space devoted to this would be useful, but it more frequently happens that the reception area is converted to a lecture space out of the normal clinic hours. This space can serve as a valuable venue for the education of clients, friends or relatives on topics that affect the community and in which the practitioner has specialist knowledge, as well as providing a space for promotional lectures to the community.

Toilets
The number of toilets on the premises should conform to the local council requirements, they should be clean and tidy and accessible to disabled clients, and it helps to have an exhaust fan linked to the light switch in the toilet.

If funds are available to take the advantages of it, one of the best forms of clinic space to acquire is an open space that can have walls installed in a way that will maximise the advantages of the space. To begin, one should not only construct a floor plan as a means of efficiently dividing the space, but also construct a ceiling plan and wall plan which allows for the planning of skylights, lighting, takes advantage of the position of existing windows and fire extinguisher sprinklers, and superimpose this onto the floor plan. This provides significant cost savings by having to avoid changing lighting and ceiling features after the walls have been erected and takes maximum advantage of sources and directions of natural light. The floor plan should also take telephone and water outlet points into consideration. Walls are preferable to partitions here, as they create a more permanent appearance. The wall cavities may be filled with acoustic barrier material if noise is an issue. Remember fire exits and the fact that a development application may have to be submitted to the local council and approved before any of this work can be done.

On a final note, if installing walls or partitions you should ensure that you allow enough room to get furniture in and out, avoid covering fire extinguisher sprinklers with partition tops, ensure that only fire resistant partitions are used and make sure that fire exits are not obstructed.

The Ideal Layout
As a means of maximising the use of space, the ideal clinic layout may look
something like the following:

The Happy Herbalist- Floor Plan

Dispensary		Toilet	Toilet
Consulting room	Corridor		Laundry
		Lecture area	
Consulting room			
		Kitchen/ library	
Consulting room			
		Reception	
	Air Lock		

Security
Consideration should also be given to the issue of clinic security. This relates to
maintaining actions and strategies that will deter burglary, break-ins and theft
from the clinic.

The issues here that relate to the clinic structure involve such things as:
• Attaching a small sign to the door stating that cash is not kept on the
  premises and drugs are not used in the clinic, or words to that effect.
• Maintaining some form of external lighting and removing or securing items
  near the clinic that could be used to assist a break-in.
• Trimming hedges or plants behind which would-be burglars may be able to
  gain entry without being seen.
• Covering door or window hinges to discourage the removal of hinge pins.
• Ensuring that some form of lighting is operating in the clinic after hours.
• Installing key-locks on windows and security grills over easily accessible
  windows situated in areas where break-ins are unlikely to be seen.
• Installing security grills on skylights.
• Installing burglar alarms.

Other issues related to security may involve:
- Not counting cash in view of clients or those with them.
- Ensuring that banking is done daily to maintain a minimal cash holding.
- Keeping the cash drawer/container open only when in use.
- Ensuring that the cash drawer/container is lockable and is locked when not in use and the key removed.
- Leave the cash drawer/ container open, empty and in plain view when the clinic is unattended to discourage burglary.
- Before leaving the clinic at the end of the day, ensure that no-one has remained on the premises.

In the event that you're faced with a person demanding money with threats of violence:
- Try to remain calm.
- Obey the persons instructions.
- Move slowly and do not invade the persons space or act in any way that may appear to be threatening.
- Take note of the persons appearance and of anything else that may assist police in their capture.
- Alert the appropriate authorities as soon as possible, close the clinic and isolate the area where the crime has taken place so that police are more easily able to conduct forensic tests.
- Ensure that anyone in the clinic who can provide further evidence either stay until police arrive or you have their contact details.
- Do not discuss with anyone outside the clinic and those who need to know, how much cash or valuables were stolen.
- Supply police with all the relevant details and consider counselling for those involved in the robbery.

Location
Assessing the Suitability of a Site
One of the most important questions that needs to be asked about the location of the clinic is, will the location have any bearing on the success of the practice? In the main, the answer to this question will be, yes. Unless one operates a mobile facility or an Internet based practice, the location will generally have a significant influence on the success of the practice. For those operating from a fixed location, serious thought should be given to where the clinic should be situated.
Consideration needs to be given to a number of factors:
- Proximity to public transport- which if it's close allows better access for those who use public transport.
- Proximity to points of referral such as health food stores, gymnasiums, pharmacies, medical practices, weight loss clinics or any other businesses that may be able to refer clients (this should be a reciprocal arrangement). It's also

beneficial to be located near a major shopping centre- people are more likely to come to the practice if the route is one which is familiar to them, and offers them an opportunity to do their shopping at the same time.

- Easy to find- it's useful to be in a position that is near well known local landmarks, so that new or potential clients can visualise your location when being given directions to the clinic, or by reading or hearing about the clinic via brochures or other marketing tools.
- Visible location- this assists when directing new clients to the clinic, and is valuable for the visibility of signage.
- Regulations related to signage- some areas have restrictions on advertising, and there may be limitations on the type and size of signs that may be used. For example, some districts which have a preponderance of older buildings will only allow signage that is in keeping with the style of those buildings.
- Ground floor premises- this makes attending the clinic easier for disabled clients.
- Prevailing winds may seem like an unusual thing to consider, but if one is inspecting a premises on a particular day and the wind is coming from the south, and the wind predominantly comes from the west, and a factory that emits large amounts of airborne waste is located to the west of the clinic, on most other days when the wind is blowing, the material emitted by the factory may be deposited on the clinic and inhaled by those in or near to it.
- Location of walls- if the proposed premises have few options regarding which rooms can be used for consultation or treatment, and the exterior walls of those rooms face west, unless those walls are shielded in some way, during summer the rooms behind them will be subject to temperatures higher than those on the other sides of the building.
- Liability-proof premises- one should look for potential public liability problems that may be associated with the premises. Surfaces that may become slippery when wet, obstacles protruding from the ground or overhead, unsupervised balconies or awkward or slippery staircases may all have the potential to cause problems.
- Availability of supplies- some rural locations and premises situated in shopping centres can provide difficulties for those delivering goods.
- Access to passing foot traffic- passing pedestrian traffic can provide an excellent means of drawing clients, and provides assistance with visibility for signage.
- Proximity to main thoroughfares- this assists client access to the clinic and assists clients' visualisation of your location.
- Attractive surroundings- these make people feel more positive about attending the clinic.
- Parking- easy access to car parking facilities is an important consideration. Undercover parking is preferred, and if this is available one should be aware of the hours of operation, parking charges, security etc, and information

should be sought from the local council regarding levies imposed upon business owners by the council for the provision of parking facilities.

- Local population characteristics- the type of people that populate your neighbourhood should be those who have the means and motivation to seek your services. This can be determined by talking with local health food and pharmacy staff, as well as other practitioners with whom you may be able to refer clients. Consideration should also be given to the notion that apparent wealth will not necessarily be associated with a high level of disposable income. It's been the experience of several practitioners that disposable income that may be spent on natural and complementary health care may be higher in working class areas than areas populated by those of higher socioeconomic classes. If, for example, one specialises in paediatric care, the local population should be strongly represented by young families. Psychographics (demographics from a psychological perspective) also need to be considered- what is the predominant attitude to your modality in the area in which you propose to practice? Much of the information that is related to these issues can be provided by the Australian Bureau of Statistics and the local council which governs the area. More will be said on this in the marketing section.

- Population density- are there enough people in the area to support the viability of the practice? For most practices operating in capital cities and the metropolitan suburban zones that surround them, unless one operates in a specialist area, these issues are not particularly critical because the population is fairly concentrated and there should usually be adequate numbers to support the clinics viability. If one plans to operate a rural practice, careful estimates need to be made regarding the level of the local population, its level of interest in your modality and its means and motivation to pursue it.

- Competition- thought needs to be given to the level of genuine competition. The term genuine is used to underline the fact that two naturopaths, two homoeopaths or two osteopaths, practicing in the same street, are not necessarily competing. If these individuals are practicing their craft in slightly different ways, and are drawing clients from different points of referral, then they may not be competing at all. There are several areas around Sydney and towns in Northern NSW where the density of practitioners is probably the highest in the country, and yet differences in modes of practice seem to allow most of these practitioners to survive and prosper without being hampered by competition.

Finally on this issue, whilst the perfect location adds a great deal of potential success to the practice, its efficiency and effectiveness, there are good examples around Australia of practitioners working in atrocious locations who are always busy, because the standard of care and clinical results that they provide enables them to overcome the impositions that may be placed upon them by a poor location.

Practice Options
Depending upon the opportunities available, a number of options exist in regard
to how one sets up a clinical practice.

Working from Home
This is an option frequently chosen by those who lack the funds to pursue
dedicated commercial premises. It's frequently used by semi-retired practitioners
or those whose clinics are not their primary sources of income. It can be difficult
to present oneself as a professional when working in this manner and for some,
the lack of separation of home and work can create problems, and it can also be
burdensome for family members or others living in the house. One has less
control over being accessed by clients, only one person who's not a normal
occupant of the house can be employed by the business, and the council needs to
be consulted regarding the zoning of the premises and whether they will allow
you to do what you wish to do in this location.

One may need to submit a development application to the council before one is
able to practice in this way, and the total amount of floor space able to be used is
normally limited to 30 square metres. In addition, the clinic space must be totally
inaccessible from any part of the house. There may also be restrictions on the use
of signs, such that the only allowable notification that can be displayed is the
street number. If the premises are being rented, the lease needs to be checked to
ensure that it allows for commercial activity. Other documents such as public
liability insurance, professional indemnity and other insurance policies also need
to be checked to ascertain whether or not they'll be affected by this activity. One
also needs to be aware that any commercial activity conducted on the premises
may influence the application of capital gains tax if the property is sold.

On the positive side, getting to work takes almost no time at all, the overall costs
are lower than many other options, there are reasonable tax advantages, and you
have a good level of control over your environment.

Sharing a Practice
Joining a group practice is a popular option. It offers advantages in being able to
network with other possibly more experienced practitioners and it's relatively cost
effective.

It may not be easy to market oneself as an individual in this environment, and the
practice standard of the other practitioners may not be the same as ones own, and
therefore, compromises may have to be made if one wants to fit in. Group
practices also have the propensity to elevate one practitioner above the others, and
the commercial success of the "non-elevatees" can suffer because of this.

Purchasing an Established Practice

Anyone pursuing this option will have a large number of issues to consider, not the least of which is the ability to fund the purchase. To this end, purchasing an existing practice can provide an immediate cash flow through an established client base and therefore repaying any borrowed funds may be somewhat easier. Staff who remain with the practice may not require retraining, and the supply lines through which one obtains therapeutic goods are already established.

Consideration needs to be given to the fact that the business has been built, and clients maintained, by someone who may have very different methods of attracting and keeping those clients who attend the clinic. If the practitioner who purchases that business departs from those methods the existing clients may not remain in the practice. In fact it's not unusual to see an existing client base fall by 30 to 50% within the first year or two of operation under the new owner.

Before considering purchasing the business, and before spending too much time carrying out a detailed and costly analysis, a superficial examination should be carried out to look for signs of poor commercial viability, these may be things such as:
• Low operating profit or cash flow.
• Problems in paying suppliers on time.
• Suppliers refusing to extend credit.
• Problems keeping to overdraft limits.
• Problems maintaining loan payments.

Further questions need to be asked when looking at this option.
• What is actually being sold? The vendor (the person selling the business) needs to provide a vendors statement, outlining the name and address of the business, the name and address of the vendor, and exactly what is being offered for sale. This may simply be the business name, it may be the rights to the lease on the property, and any leases on equipment, rights of access to clients, and ownership of stock, fixtures, fittings and all intellectual property. Whether or not one chooses to buy the entire package on offer should also be considered- this may be able to be negotiated with the vendor. It should also be ascertained whether or not the things on offer can actually be sold.
• Are the fixtures and fittings subject to finance? If so, their real value needs to be shown.
• Can any of the leases involved actually be transferred? The details of the tenancy lease and its expiry date, if the premises are leased, need to be known. It may be that another party has the first option on the premises once the current lease expires, or the landlord is not planning on re-offering the property for lease after it expires.

- Is the outgoing practitioner planning on taking the existing telephone number with them? You should ensure that the telephone number is acquired if you go ahead with the purchase.
- Does the lease-holder have to cover the costs of external cleaning or maintenance? If so, this should be factored into the costs of running the practice.
- Does the current lease allow you to do what you want to do? Clearance to practice should be obtained in writing from the landlord.
- Are any staff who stay with the business due for long service, annual or maternity leave? Remember that leave entitlements are continuous if staff stay with the business.
- Is any particular staff member critical to the success of the business? If so, are they staying or leaving with the outgoing practitioner?
- Are the policies and procedures used by the clinic consistent with your preferred method of operating? If not, staff may need to be retrained, and clients may need to be handled in the manner that they've become used to until you can bring your own methods into play.
- Are any new developments planned for the local area? The local council should be contacted in regard to the development of any new businesses, roads or anything else that may have an impact upon the future of the clinic
- Will you be able to operate the type of business you want on these premises? This needs to be confirmed in writing by the local council, and it may be that a development application needs to be lodged with the council. This will involve a fee of between $50 and $100 and the application may take several weeks to process.
- Has the current practitioner adhered to the conditions of the lease? If the premises are leased or rented the agent should be asked to carry out an inspection on the property to ensure that the lease agreement hasn't been breached by any additions to the premises or anything else that may contravene the lease agreement.
- If goodwill is involved in the sale price, is it properly valued? Goodwill is a relatively subjective figure, based loosely around the businesses reputation and the ability of the business to generate future revenue. One may need the services of an independent accountant to verify that the goodwill figure is realistic.
- If stock, fixtures and fittings are being sold as part of a package, are they properly valued? Has any previously claimed depreciation been factored into these valuations?
- If dispensary stock is being sold, how was it valued? How much of its shelf life still exists? Has any of it already been sold to clients and is awaiting collection? Is the stocktake being done at the time of sale or before? Is any of the stock subject to lease or finance? Is the current stock-holding too high- can it be reduced? Can the price be negotiated? Is this stock that you would normally prescribe if given the opportunity? The salient points here are that

the value and level of stock should be correct at the time of the sale, and it should be stock that you can and would normally use. What you buy here should be open to negotiation or consideration should be given to excluding it from the purchase of the business if it doesn't suit your requirements.

- Is the practice currently trading with suppliers under any restrictive terms? If a business has difficulty paying its bills on time, suppliers may withdraw the normal credit allowances and restrict trading to cash transactions only. This may cause problems for the new owner, who should contact the suppliers in question and inform them of the change of ownership.
- How successful has the business been to date? A statement from the vendor as to the trading record of the business should be provided, and/or a statement from a chartered public accountant setting out the relevant financial details for at least the past 3 years. These details need careful examination to confirm that the profitability of the business has been going up rather than down. If the business operates as a limited liability company, you need to know if you're assuming any risk or liability through the actions of the previous owner. Bank records may need to be matched against the client appointment book to confirm that what appears to be income has not been channelled into the businesses bank account from sources other than the clinic, thereby artificially inflating income figures to make the business appear more attractive. One also needs to confirm that bad debts arising from the injudicious use of credit or the acceptance of bouncing cheques and has not been calculated as income, and thereby falsely inflating income figures. Does the business have any outstanding debts that are not shown on the accounts?
- Are all expenses shown? Has the vendor paid for expenses from money from other sources, thereby diminishing the level of apparent expenses? Has the vendor delayed paying some expenses as a means of artificially reducing the expense level? Are some expenses about to be increased? Have some expenses been prepaid by the vendor as a means of reducing the apparent expense level, and for which you'll have to reimburse them?
- Are any large regular payments (telephone, power etc) due to be paid soon after the transfer of the business?
- Is the business subject to any negligence, malpractice or civil claims?
- Is the business free of all encumbrances and claims by creditors or clients?
- Are the warranties for service on any items subject to the sale transferable? Warranty agreements for some equipment may be confined to the original purchaser, and if this was the practitioner rather than the business, these may not be transferable.
- Why is the business being sold? It needs to be clearly shown that the business is not being sold because of poor commercial performance, or for some other reason that will negatively impact upon its future.
- Does the outgoing practitioner plan to open another clinic nearby? As a means of discouraging this, the sale contract should contain a restraint of trade or exclusion clause, stipulating that the practitioner shall not operate a

clinic within a certain radius of the existing clinic, for a set period of time-
this may be within a 20 km radius for a period of 10 years for example.
- Have stamp duties, security deposits or bonds, development application
costs, legal and other fees been factored into the purchase price? Does the
business still look like a viable proposition once these costs are considered?
- Can you sustain the possible drop in clientele once the clientele realise that
the former practitioner no longer operates in the practice? As means of
reducing this loss, it may be advisable to ask the original practitioner to stay
on in the practice for a fixed period, say 3 months, so that existing clients
have the opportunity to see the new practitioner with the old practitioner. In
most circumstances, this association of the familiar with the unfamiliar can
facilitate a smoother transfer and engender some transfer of trust.

The list of questions above may seem overly cautious, but it's best to be well
aware of the potential problems long before one is legally committed to the
acquisition of the business.

Before negotiating the purchase of the business, it's often useful to draft an offer
statement, outlining what you want to offer, and the clauses and conditions that
you'd like to insert in the sale contract (mentioned below). This serves as a
starting point for negotiations.

The sale itself should be carried out using a sale contract, which again clearly
defines what is being sold and who is selling it. If either party defaults on any part
of the contract they may be subject to financial penalties resulting from legal
claims by the aggrieved party. If you elect to purchase the business and you need
finance to do this, the sale contract should stipulate that the purchase is subject to
finance. If the approval of any local or state authority is still pending or it's still
unclear if the lease allows you to practice in the way that you wish to, the sale
contract should be marked, subject to the successful receipt or transfer of all
licences and permissions to trade. You may also wish to consider marking the sale
contract, subject to the receipt of copies of all requested financial records, as an
incentive for full disclosure of these items. It also needs to be remembered that
commercial rents are subject to GST, and the purchaser of the business has to pay
the stamp duty on the transfer of the business and that the cost of the stamp duty
is based on the total value of the sale, including stock.

Should the sale go ahead, the ATO needs to be notified of the change of
ownership, and if the business is a limited company, the Australian Securities and
Investments Commission should also be notified of the change of ownership. If
the practice is located in Victoria, the purchaser and vendor should also be aware
of the requirements stipulated in the Health Records Act 2001 (Victoria)- see the
section headed Exit and Succession Planning, later in this book for more on this
issue.

Because of the large number of issues that need to be dealt with in this situation, the acquisition and change-over of the business can be coordinated relatively smoothly by the use of a transfer plan. This is a step-wise plan or flow chart outlining the tasks that should be performed, the order in which they should be performed and the dates by which these tasks need to be completed.

A practitioner selling a clinic should also obviously be aware of all of the issues mentioned above.

Buying Commercial Premises and Establishing your Own Practice
This is an expensive method of starting a practice, and whilst it's not unheard of, it's relatively rare. It is however one of the best methods of maximising the control over one's surroundings and the costs involved ensure that one is always highly motivated towards success.

Establishing your Own Practice in Leased or Rented Premises
This is a location option commonly selected by those who are committed to developing a successful practice but do not have the funds to be able to purchase the premises at the outset. Once the general location has been selected, one can then begin to examine individual properties that are suitable for leasing. As a means of saving time, it may be appropriate to brief local real estate agencies on what you're looking for, let the agents look for you and check recommended premises. It's also useful to ask local agents about average rental prices for the area selected so that the amount of expense that will be incurred is known.

One would be well advised to treat this exercise as if one were buying the property. The amount of time and money that normally goes into establishing a business is significant, and problems with the building or surrounds that may result in moving to other premises can be very costly. A building inspection by someone who's licensed to carry out this task, done before the lease is signed, can provide a good level of insurance against the unknown, such as faulty wiring that may cause fire or structural problems that may cause injury or ill health to staff or clients. One should beware that low rents or premises that have been on the market for some time may be associated with problems with the premises or their surrounds.

For those of an impetuous nature, if one sees a property that one desires on first sight, it may be wise to ask the agent for the first option on the property and keep looking, and be aware that some documents headed, "Intention to Lease", may actually bind you to the lease. A lease should never be signed until you know that you can actually practice what you want to in the premises. A lease should not be signed after only one inspection- a second or third inspection can reveal problems that were not noticed during the first. Think carefully about leasing premises within shopping centres, as the lease conditions on these types of premises may make allowance for the owner to move you to other parts of the centre, or impose other conditions that restrict your ability to operate.

One should determine what types of lease options are available and choose whichever is suitable with the appropriate option at the expiry of the lease period. For example, this may be a 3 year lease with an option for a further 3 years.

One should be aware that properties which are still held in a mortgage can be sold if the owner cannot maintain the mortgage repayments. If this occurs, there are no guarantees that the new owner will want to maintain the lease. Because the lease agreement is with the previous owner, the new owner is not bound by the agreement. Therefore it's useful to get the mortgagee, i.e. the bank etc, to sign a consent to lease contract, with the same terms and conditions as those signed with the agent.

Read the lease document carefully and note such things as the frequency of rental reviews, which may allow the agent to periodically increase the rent. Note whether or not the lease-holder is responsible for maintenance, cleaning or rubbish removal, whether or not the local council imposes any levies on parking, the hours of operation that the lease allows, and whether the lease allows you the option of purchasing the property. Rental reviews may be linked to rises in the CPI (Consumer Price Index), or increases in the market value of the property.

It may also be useful to determine if the lease allows for subletting to other practitioners, as this may be something that you'd like the option of doing in the future.

After an adequate inspection has been made of the premises, written agreement to make any necessary repairs should be sought from the agent prior to signing the lease, and the repairs preferably carried out prior to taking up the lease. There's no reason why attempts should not be made to negotiate the value of the rent, and the lease agreement should be signed with "subject to the receipt of all licences and permissions to trade", "subject to finance", "subject to agreed repairs being carried out", "subject to approval of development application" or with any other condition that you feel is appropriate.

Buying and Operating a Health Food Store
Given the nature of the business, this option is really only suitable for a naturopath, and even then, it's not a particularly good choice. Whilst the access to potential clients may be excellent, the conversion of a conversation about someone's health problem on the shop floor to a paid consultation is a difficult task. In the main, customers are reluctant to become clients, feeling that they can save the time and money by getting what they want on the shop floor, and client follow up interviews often occur over the counter rather than in the consulting

room. It needs to be borne in mind here that professional consultations can only take place in a separate area designed for this purpose. Client perceptions of practitioners operating in this manner may be that the practitioner is less professional than one operating in a dedicated clinic. The only real advantages here are that it may take less time for the business to break even, the income from retail products may be quite good, and customers value the advice of a retailer who is a trained practitioner. Unfortunately, the majority of practitioners who embark on such a course eventually cease clinical practice to concentrate on the retail business.

Working in a Health Food Store or Pharmacy
Again, this option is really only suitable for a naturopath. Naturopaths are often hired to lend credibility to the business- it may be that the practitioner is hired to work on the shop floor to promote sales as well as consult in designated premises, either way, given that this a retail environment, one's selling skills need to be fairly good.

When getting started, these locations can provide good training grounds for the honing of communication and self-promotion skills, and are a good means of becoming known in the neighbourhood. One thing to bear in mind here is that the customers who come to the business should be allowed to stay with the business- it is not appropriate to poach the pharmacy's or health food store's customers. This method of work should only be viewed as a short-term option. As with owning a health food store, working in this environment also has a negative impact on the perception of the practitioner as a professional. In both of these venues, salary, commissions and working conditions may need to be negotiated, so it's wise to talk to other practitioners working in this industry to determine what can realistically be expected.

Operating a Mobile Practice
Operating a mobile or outcall practice essentially means that the practitioner goes to the client rather than the other way around. This obviously provides for lower running costs, but the establishment of the business may involve the purchase of a vehicle. In most cases this may not be the best way to present oneself professionally.

One should be aware of public liability issues arising from this type of practice. For example if the practitioner injures themselves on a clients premises the client would normally be liable but claims on a clients insurance may cause problems that can be averted if one carried one's own public liability insurance. Finally, it has been the experience of several practitioners that payment before the treatment or consultation is preferable to payment afterwards, and the fees charged for out calls are generally $10 - $15 above the normal in-clinic fee.

8. Clinic Management
Payment and Receipts
Fees for Professional Services

Statistics indicate that as a profession, non-medical healthcare practitioners are frequently somewhat relaxed about setting realistic fees. Someone once said that a business essentially consists of three elements- product, service and price, and that it was unwise to attempt to be the best in all three areas. Pricing as it relates to non-medical healthcare is not as sensitive as in, say, real estate, grocery or other areas of commerce. The areas that tend to receive more attention from the marketplace are clinical outcomes and the quality of the services provided. Pricing, within certain parameters, tends to receive less attention, and as such, one can afford to set one's fees at or indeed somewhat above, the local average. In addition to this, it is fairly well known that a significant section of the marketplace tends to associate low price with a poor quality product, and a certain aura of prestige may be associated with a high fee structure.

Opposing this is the fact that by setting one's fees too high, one may exclude those who do not have the capacity to pay, thereby denying that section of the community access to the results that your services may be able to provide. One also needs to consider that an appropriate fee structure should cover the costs of operating the business and also provide an appropriate level of remuneration for the practitioner. The level at which fees are set needs to take all of these things into consideration, as well as the level of rebate provided by healthcare insurers. Money Success and You by John Kehoe, mentioned in the Suggested Texts section above, provides useful discussion on these issues.

There are several methods of determining what constitutes a reasonable fee.
1. One of the most common is to determine the local average and set one's fees somewhere around the mean. This may be a mean of $65 for the first consultation with a range of $45 to $85, and a mean of $35 for a follow-up consultation with a range of $25 to $45. It may not be unreasonable then to set the initial consultation fee at $70, and follow-up consultations at $40. Once again, if one provides efficient and effective clinical outcomes backed up by good quality service, there's less reason to adhere too closely to the community mean.
2. Another method which is occasionally applied is to relate the fee structure to the weekly return on the investment that has been made both in the business (this does not include the cost of purchasing the dispensary) and in one's professional training, including the weekly running costs, added to the amount of weekly income desired, and dividing this by the number clients that one can comfortably see in a week. As an example, the original investment in the business may have been $10,000, the cost of professional training $30,000, and calculating an annual rate of return of 20% gives a weekly return of $153.85. The weekly running costs (this includes the total costs of a receptionist) may be $1000. This total of $1153.85, added to a gross desired income of $1000, provides a total per

week of $2153.85. If one were to be able to comfortably deal with 50 clients per week, then the fee averages between first and follow-up consultations would be $2153.85 divided by 50, which is $43.08. Using these figures, one could conceivably set one's fees at the level given in example one, considering that once the business has been running for some time, the bulk of the consultations would be follow-ups. This example ignores the sales of dispensary items, as the mark-up on these products allows them to be self-funding and a separate cost and revenue area (more will be said on this later).

It should be kept in mind here that unless one is purchasing an ongoing business with an established clientele it will take some time to build the client load to the 50 clients per week mentioned in the examples.

Fee Increases
Consideration should be given to regular increases in fees. Various government departments calculate the quarterly and annual increases in the cost of living, and these increases are reflected by the CPI. The CPI affects everyone, client and practitioner alike. Therefore, as your costs increase, so should the fees you need to charge to pay for these increased costs. As a rough guide, fees should be increased annually in line with increases in the CPI. Other reasons for fee increases may occur and these may be things such as a significant rise in the cost of a frequently used therapeutic good, or some other issue that may lead to an increase in practice costs. In these cases fees should be increased to meet the economic effects of these events. For more on this and other issues related to fees and how to view them realistically, see John Kehoe's Money Success and You, mentioned earlier.

Payment
The only person handling fees should be the receptionist. Unless it's unavoidable (such as in the case of home visits) the practitioner should not be handling fees. There are essentially two forms of relationship that the client has with the practice- a therapeutic relationship and a commercial relationship. These relationships should be clearly delineated and handled by different people. If this separation does not happen the two issues can become mixed, the therapeutic relationship can become altered, and the quality of that relationship may be adversely affected.

As part of the payment options it's important to provide clients with access to credit card and EFTPOS facilities. The provision of these services needs to be established with your bank of choice, and because a telephone line is necessary to carry out the funds transfer, consideration may need to be given to the installation of a new phone line. A monthly fee (around $25) is normally charged by the bank to maintain the facility and a fee of between 1 and 2 percent of gross turnover is also payable, although this turnover percentage may be able to be negotiated with the bank. As a rule, it's not advisable to take cheques for the payment of fees. Extending credit to a client is a matter of personal choice, but it has the potential to create even more problems than cheques, and should be avoided.

As a matter of courtesy, clients should be told about payment options as well as the cost of the consultation and possible therapeutic goods costs at the time of booking the consultation. To reinforce this, a scale of fees and therapeutic goods costs should be prominently displayed on or near the reception desk.

Bad Debt
Bad debt refers to non cash payments that do not result in a transfer of funds. They are most commonly caused by payments by cheque where the account has insufficient funds to meet the face value of the cheque. Although bad debts are uncommon in the non-medical healthcare industry, care should be taken with cheques and as mentioned earlier, their use as a means of payment should be discouraged.

Float
Enough cash of differing denominations should be kept on the premises to provide change for those clients paying cash, for one days' trading. The amount and type of each denomination held will be influenced by the number of clients seen in a day, the prices charged for consultations and any therapeutic goods prescribed. For example, if the consultations happened to be $70 and $45 and no medicines or other goods were ever provided, the predominant denomination in the float should be $5 notes, with a lesser amount of $10 an $20 notes for those paying for the $70 consultation with a $100 note. Therefore, if one routinely saw no more than 10 clients per day, and these were mostly for follow-up consultations, and paying $45 for the consultation, then a float consisting of ten $5 notes, five $10 notes and five $20 notes should be adequate for the day.

If medicines etc were priced at $9.95, $19.95, $24.95 and so on, and every client received between 1 and 3 medicines, the float should carry enough 5 cent coins to deal with those clients who pay cash in even dollars, and enough 10 and 20 cent coins to cover change for those clients who pay the dollar fractions in coins. Typically, if a maximum of 10 clients are seen in a day, the float may consist of ten 50 cent coins (and an appropriate number of smaller denomination coins depending upon the prices of goods sold), ten 1 dollar coins, ten 2 dollar coins, ten 5 dollar notes, five 20 dollar notes and two 50 dollar notes. It's also useful to make arrangements with another business located nearby that can supply change if required.

The money used to make up the float should not be taken from the current days takings except to make up change. Failure to observe this often results in confusion about where money used for the float has come from, and mixing the float with the income can confuse the income figures for that day. An effort should be made to keep all other cash separated from the float as this will minimise the loss if a robbery is attempted.

Receipts
Receipts for services provided and any goods supplied must be given to the client at the end of the consultation. A typical receipt may look like the following:

Tax Receipt				

The Happy Herbalist
Receipt No:.....................
Norman Happy DBM.
10 Helianthus Drive
Happy Hill Qld 4006
Ph/Fax 07-31190004
Prov. No. J99904A
ABN 99 777 001 555
www.happy.com.au

For Professional Services
For (Client details including address)
....
....

Service or Goods Provided	Item Number	Cost	GST	Total
Total				

....
Paid
....
Date

The receipt should carry all of the details shown in the example above, including the WorkCover provider number if one exists. The service or goods provided section should outline what was provided (naturopathic consult, homoeopathic consult etc). The item number refers to the item number given to the product or service by the clients healthcare insurance provider. Cost refers to the cost of the service or goods without GST, the GST is as stated, and the total next to the GST refers to the cost plus GST of each service or item. The total referred to at the bottom refers to totals of each of the cost, GST and total columns. The receipt should be signed and dated by the receptionist and a copy kept with the clients' file. Some practices also list the method of payment on the receipt, whether this is by cash or credit card etc, and consideration should also be given to the inclusion of the clinic logo beside or near the clinic details. The practitioner named on the receipt should be the one who performed the service and if a group consultation is performed, separate receipts should be issued to each client. Provider numbers as issued by the clients healthcare insurance provider and the clinics ABN should also be shown. Receipts should be numbered sequentially.

Client Interview Forms
Initial Interview Form
There a number of different types of client interview forms, and the variations will largely be influenced by the modality practiced by the practitioner. For example, those practitioners working mainly in the areas of nutrition and dietetics should devote a significant amount of space on the form to recording dietary details. Those working with physical and manipulative therapies will be concentrating more in the areas of musculoskeletal function, and the interview form should reflect this bias. Interview forms used by homoeopaths, naturopaths, herbalists and other practitioners taking a more general view of the clients' health will reflect this general view.

As a means of economising the clients as well as the practitioners time, it's useful to have the client fill in some of their details (the area under "Client Details" only) while waiting for the consultation to begin.

An example of an initial client interview form which may take this more general view follows. As with the receipt, the practitioner named on the form must be the one carrying out the consultation.

The Happy Herbalist Form Norman Happy DBM. 10 Helianthus Drive Happy Hill Qld 4006 Ph/Fax 07-31190004 Prov. No. J99904A ABN 99 777 001 555 www.happy.com.au	Client Initial Interview		
Client Details (please use block capitals) Today's date...			
.... Surname	.... Christian names	.... Date of birth	.... Sex (male or female)
.... Nationality .... Address	.... Phone at home .... Phone at work .... Marital status	.... Health insurance Co. .... e-mail address .... Number of children	
.... Regular Medical Doctor	.... Date of last visit to doctor	.... Your occupation	
.... Medication currently being used including all natural medicines- please include dose used.			
.... Allergies			
.... How did you hear about our practice?			
For office use only. Please do not fill in any of the spaces below.			
Medical history (including recent and past surgery)			

Current signs and symptoms

....

....

....

Aggravating or Ameliorating factors

....

Iridology Analysis

....

Menstrual Cycle

....

Immunisation History

....

Lifestyle History

....

Client Perceived Obstacles to Wellness (money, time, lack of commitment etc)

....

....

Current General Wellness Rating (out of 10)...

....	....	....	....	....
Blood pressure	Pulse rate	Respiratory rate	Temperature	Reflexes

Regular Daily Diet			
....	....	....	....
....	....	....	....
....	....	....	....
....	....	....	....
Breakfast	Lunch	Dinner	Snacks

73

```
Recovery Plan
General
..............................................................................................................
..............................................................................................................
..............................................................................................................
..............................................................................................................
..............................................................................................................

Herbal Medicine
..............................................................................................................
..............................................................................................................

Nutritional Supplements
..............................................................................................................
..............................................................................................................

Homoeopathy
..............................................................................................................
..............................................................................................................

Diet
..............................................................................................................
..............................................................................................................

Exercise and Lifestyle
..............................................................................................................
..............................................................................................................
..............................................................................................................
..............................................................................................................

Next Appointment Date...............................................................
```

It's possible to construct extraordinarily complex interview forms that list all of the body systems (respiratory, gastrointestinal etc) as a reminder for review, as well as including an exhaustive list of diseases that the client may have or have had, that can be ticked off while the client fills in the top of the form. Whilst these may be useful for those new to clinical practice, they can be time consuming to fill out, particularly when that time may be better spent establishing rapport and concentrating on the main reason for the client attending the clinic.

These forms can also be tailored to add questions of special interest such as whether or not the client has amalgam dental fillings, family history and to include areas relating to specific diagnostic modalities such as iridology, electro-dermal testing and live blood analysis.

Ultimately, the initial interview form should be designed around the way the practitioner prefers to practice and whether the practitioner has a memory that does or doesn't require a checklist. Copies of all dietary and other advice sheets and all other written material provided to the client should also be attached to the interview form.

Some specific areas to note on these forms are those headed "Client perceived obstacles to wellness" and "Current general wellness". Details recorded under these headings, even though somewhat subjective, can provide useful guides to future recovery programs and the clients progress through the recovery process.

Follow-up Interview Form
The follow-up consultation form will normally be less voluminous that the initial interview form due to the reduction in historical focus and concentration on the current situation. An example of a follow-up client interview form which may take a general view may look something like this:

The Happy Herbalist	Client Follow-Up Interview Form

The Happy Herbalist   Client Follow-Up Interview Form
Norman Happy DBM.
10 Helianthus Drive
Happy Hill Qld 4006
Ph/Fax 07-31190004
Prov. No. J99904A
ABN 99 777 001 555
www.happy.com.au

Client Details (please use block capitals)
Today's date...

....	....	....
Surname	Christian names	Date of birth

....

....
Medication currently being used including all natural medicines. Please include dose used.

For office use only. Please do not fill in any of the spaces below.

Present signs and symptoms
....

....
Client Perceived Continuing Obstacles to Wellness
....

....
Current General Wellness Rating (out of 10)...............

....	....	....	....	....
Blood pressure	Pulse rate	Respiratory rate	Temperature	.... Reflexes

Regular Daily Diet

....	....	....	....

....	....	....	....
Breakfast	Lunch	Dinner	Snacks

Updated Recovery Plan
General

....
....

Herbal Medicine

....

Nutritional Supplements

....

Homoeopathy

....

Diet

....

Exercise and Lifestyle

....
....

Next Appointment Date...

As with the previous form, the practitioner named on the form must be the one carrying out the consultation. Again, copies of any written communication provided to the client must be attached to this form and this should be attached to the initial interview form and all other data related to the client. Note that the clients name and date of birth should be filled out on this form as well as the initial interview form. The reason for this is that it has frequently occurred that a practitioner may be dealing with two different people with the same name, and in the event that the follow-up form becomes detached from the main body of paperwork, much time can be saved when trying to discover who the real client is by simply adding the date of birth. The repeated request for medication information can assist in monitoring client compliance with the medication advice given in the previous consultation.

Specialised or Dedicated Interview Forms
If one specialises in a particular area, forms may be designed to be filled out during or prior to the consultation that can be used as a basis for discussion in the consultation. For example, an interview carried out by a practitioner specialising in the management of depression may be expedited by the use of a form such as the following.

The Happy Herbalist Norman Happy DBM. 10 Helianthus Drive Happy Hill Qld 4006 Ph/Fax 07-31190004 Prov. No. J99904A ABN 99 777 001 555 www.happy.com.au	Client Emotional Checklist Form		
Client Name:	Date:		
Please place a tick in the space that you feel best answers the following questions			
	Every now and then	Some of the time	All the time
I feel sad or depressed			
I wake early in the morning for no obvious reason			
I rarely feel like eating			
I'm losing weight			
I feel like a valuable member of the community			
I like the company of others			
My life is heading in the direction I'd like it to			
I feel like I'm in control of my life			
I'm tired for no reason			
I feel as if other people would be better off if I were dead			
My life is as enjoyable as it always was			
I make decisions easily			
My mind functions as well as it always has			
I feel irritable			
Things that used to be important now feel pointless			

By tallying up the responses and working out an arbitrary score on a form such as this, relatively rapid determinations can be made about the need for treatment.

Policies and Procedures
Part of the means by which businesses survive and do so successfully is through the use of planned and consistent actions. Planned responses can be formalised through the use of set policies and procedures. Essentially, a policy is a fixed position on a certain subject, and a procedure details the method by which that policy is put into action. The application of carefully considered policies and

procedures promotes smooth, efficient and professional management of the practice.

Policies
A policy is a fixed and consistent position on a specific aspect of the practice activity, and may relate to the question, "what do we do if?" How this question is answered will be determined by our values, principles, ethics and commercial aims. These answers are then formalised into policies.

Policies may be divided into the areas of external relations, strategic planning, administration, client management, staffing, buildings and equipment and policies relating the financial matters. Policy manuals provide excellent guidelines for staff and can be very useful as training manuals for new staff or locums. They also act as a means of insurance against rash or ill-considered responses to problems, and refine the decision making process.

Following are some of the areas where fixed policies can be useful.
- What do you do if a client is late?
- What do you do if someone asks you to treat cancer, diabetes or HIV AIDS?
- What do you do if you suspect that a child is being abused by one of its parents?
- What do you do if it becomes clear that one of your clients wants to commit suicide?
- What do you do if you make a clients condition worse and they want to take legal action against you?
- What do you do if a client fails to show up for an appointment?
- What do you do if you're targeted by the media for some reason?
- What do you do if you become ill on a Sunday night, are unable to attend the clinic, and you're fully booked for the next week?
- What do you do if you have a power failure?
- What do you do if you have a fire?
- What do you do if your reception computer crashes?
- What do you do if you've double booked clients?
- What do you do if a client has an acute asthmatic attack, heart attack or experiences some other potentially fatal incident while on the premises?
- What's your policy on fees, concessions and increases etc?
- What's your policy on equipment upgrades?
- What's your policy on staff training?

The policy manual should be reviewed regularly and updated when required, and kept in a central site for easy access. The principal practitioner in the clinic should know all of the policies and all their accompanying procedures.

Procedures
Procedures are the methods by which policies are carried out. For example, in the event that the practitioner is incapacitated and unable to consult with clients, the policy may be that the nominated locum (whose name and contact details should be clearly written in the policies and procedures manual) services the clients until the practitioner is fit for work. The accompanying procedure might look something like the following:
1. No new bookings should be taken during the principal practitioners' period of incapacity.
2. The nominated locum should be contacted as soon as possible and asked to service booked clients for this period.
3. In the event that the nominated locum cannot attend, all clients who are scheduled to attend the clinic during the practitioners' absence shall be telephoned as early as possible and rescheduled for a later date.
4. Any clients requiring urgent attention during this period should be booked in to see other nominated practitioners (the names and contact details for these practitioners should be clearly written in the policy and procedures manual).

It's useful to get staff involved in writing procedures as doing so may engender a sense of ownership of the task. Normally, the procedure will accompany the policy to which it relates, and the whole bound into a single manual.

Non-policy Procedures
There should also be a record of the methods by which normal activities are carried out. Again, this assists everyone involved in the task, and particularly new staff or locums. These types of procedures should cover things such as medicine re-ordering levels, stocktake methods, telephone answering techniques, the details of tradespeople who can be called upon to carry out specific maintenance and so on.

Professional Report Writing
The occasion will frequently arise where you need to refer a client for a second opinion or further treatment and a report needs to accompany the client when they see the next practitioner. This may be particularly relevant in the case of WorkCover clients, where the WorkCover Authority may require a report on the progress of clients under your care.

There are normally set elements to a professional report, and these normally consist of what you found, what you did, why you did it and when you did it. The events outlined should be dated and kept in chronological order, the entire report should be made on the clinic letterhead and signed and dated by the practitioner who carried out the treatment. The writing style should be determined by who is expected to read it, and a copy of the report should be kept in the clients' file.

Reception Techniques
Initial Telephone Contact
Telephone techniques used by the receptionist should, as much as possible, be standardised. The procedure should minimise time and maximise the quality of contact and the use of the information exchanged between the receptionist and the caller. It should be remembered here that the generation of new business by the practice is heavily dependent upon the quality of the initial contact between a potential client and the clinic, and the ability of the receptionist to convert the enquiry into a booking. Most of this initial contact occurs through the telephone. Significant and long-lasting impressions can be created in the first few seconds of telephone contact and they can greatly influence the outcome of the call as well as the long term relationship between the clinic and the client.

 A great deal has been written on successful telephone techniques, and whilst it's difficult to standardise a conversation where almost anything may be said by the caller, the method described below should maximise the potential of the telephone enquiry.

Firstly, the telephone should be answered within 3 rings. Any delay past this point may indicate to the caller something less than efficiency. Having picked up the call, the receptionist should then wait briefly for any long distance or mobile phone pips to play out before speaking. Much of the greeting used to answer the phone can be drowned out by these pips, and the effect of a carefully crafted telephone greeting lost.

The phone should be answered with a standard response, for example, "Thank you for calling the Happy Herbalist, this is Norma." One of the main points to note here is that the last word that the caller hears in this answer is the name of the person they're talking with- this promotes more effective communication. It should also be noted that the name of the clinic is identified early, so that the caller is reassured that they have rung the correct number. The receptionist's tone should be friendly but efficient, respectful but professional, as well as positive and reassuring.

The caller should then be allowed to state the reason for the call, and the receptionist should clearly and succinctly respond with the appropriate information, again in a courteous, friendly and reassuring fashion. It should be remembered here that the callers time is valuable, and they may not appreciate verbose responses the questions that are capable of being answered more efficiently. As to the content of this ensuing conversation,

- The callers health problems should not be discussed at any length during this conversation, apart from that which is necessary to assure that caller that help can be provided and the appointment secured. Lengthy discussions at this point have the potential to undermine the future relationship with the practitioner. Without the training to carry on such a conversation, it also has the potential to reduce the credibility and perceived professionalism of the practice.
- The caller should be reassured that the services requested can be provided by the clinic, and if they cannot, the caller should be referred to an appropriate practice, which should offer reciprocal referrals.
- Once the services that the caller requires have been identified, the costs of those services should be outlined, the caller asked if they have insurance cover for these services, and they should be told about the rebate system for these services. (Rebate schedules should be kept near the phone)
- The caller should be told about the clinic policy regarding payment, and whether or not cheques or credit cards or any barter system points can be used to pay for the services.
- The caller should be told how long the services required should take, and be asked to bring any relevant diagnostic reports, information on current therapies or any other pertinent documentation.
- During this conversation, it is useful if the receptionist can determine if the potential client requires assistance with stress, anxiety or some form of emotional problem, in which case the interview may require somewhat more time than usual. This being the case, attempts should be made to schedule this client in as the last appointment of the day, to minimise the potential disturbance caused to the days schedule if the interaction requires more time, and to allow more time for the interaction.
- If the caller needs to be placed on hold, one should be aware that since the clients and the clinics time is valuable, these moments should not be wasted. On hold tapes outlining the features and benefits of the practice, and the modalities practiced (similar to those outlined in the clinic brochures discussed later) can be used to great advantage. Whilst on-hold music or radio broadcasts may at times be soothing, they make little use of this valuable time.
- At some point early in the conversation, without diminishing the voiced concern for the persons wellbeing, they should be asked where they heard about the clinic, and this noted on a marketing media monitoring form.
- Once the callers commitment to treatment has been secured, they should be asked when they'd like to attend the practice. It's important here to be aware that if the caller is offered any time at all on any day, the impression may be given that the clinic has no clients and perhaps the clinical outcomes produced in the practice may not be very good. The caller should be asked

what day they'd prefer, and then, in the case where no other bookings have been made for that day, offered one of two possibilities- one time in the morning and one time in the afternoon. As the bookings for this particular day start to increase, subsequent clients should be booked so that the appointments are back to back, rather than staggered with gaps in between. As clients arrive at the clinic, other clients coming and going gives a much better impression than one in which the receptionist and the sole client for the next 4 hours are the only people present in the reception area. Gaps between clients can also have a negative effect on the enthusiasm levels of both the practitioner and the receptionist.

- Once the appointment is booked, the receptionist should ensure that they have the all of the relevant client details- surname and Christian names, home and work contact phone numbers, the services requested and the callers health insurance fund details.
- The caller should then be asked how they're getting to the clinic, and be given directions to the clinic as they relate to the mode of transport used by the client. If coming by private vehicle they should be told about parking facilities and the hours of operation of those facilities and any costs involved. If coming by public transport they should be told where the nearest pick up/departure points are located. The person should be asked to repeat these directions if the receptionist has any concerns about the callers understanding of the directions.

In closing, the caller should be thanked for contacting the clinic (using the name of the clinic as a reminder), reminded to bring all of their relevant documentation, told that they'll be contacted on the day before the appointment to confirm their attendance, and reminded of the date and time of their appointment.

The receptionist should be well versed in this procedure, and it should be written out and kept near the reception area for use by any temporary receptionists who may be employed by the practice. This method of reception may also be modified for use when people come in off the street to enquire about the services offered by the clinic.

When Arriving at the Clinic
When the client comes into the clinic for their appointment, reception should follow a procedure essentially designed to welcome and calm them. The mechanics of this procedure normally consist of the receptionist greeting the client (using the clients' name), introducing themselves and welcoming them to the clinic. If the client is on time it's useful to thank them for this as it encourages further punctuality. It's then advisable to let the client know if the practitioner is running to schedule and if the client has to wait for more than 5 minutes for the consultation they may be offered a cup of tea or some other form of refreshment.

They should then be given the client interview form and a pen and asked to fill in the appropriate details whilst waiting in the reception area.

When the consultation is about to begin the practitioner should collect the client from the reception area after introducing themselves, and lead the client to the consulting room. On completion of the consultation the practitioner should thank the client for coming and ensure that they have received the appropriate treatment, advice sheets and promotional information. The client should be told when they need to come in to the clinic again and the receptionist should be asked to make the appropriate booking at a time suitable to the client and the clinic. The booking register should then be filled in accordingly, the client given an appointment/business card listing the clinic details, with the date and time clearly listed along with the practitioner they're due to see. The client should then told that they will receive a reminder call 24 hours prior to the appointment.

Cleaning

The job of cleaning the clinic should not be done by the receptionist but should be done by local professional cleaners or the practitioner. If carpet is used in the clinic, steam cleaning every 3-6 months is a good investment. Cleanliness is an occupational health and safety requirement, and a clean and professional appearance adds to the overall attraction of the clinic.

Data Storage

Healthcare clinics amass large amounts of data- financial records, dispensary records, client files and clinical reports. As mentioned earlier, it's essential to keep copies of some of this material off site, but this isn't always possible. The area where this can be most difficult is that of client records. Whilst material such as pathology reports and X-rays may not be easily convertible to an electronic format, where possible, client interview details should be stored electronically and copies kept off-site.

The only major potential risk here is the possibility of a clinic computer malfunction or power blackout, rendering the files inaccessible. This problem may be overcome by maintaining a backup, battery powered notebook or laptop computer, with sufficient processing power and memory to handle the activities of the clinic. If this back-up system is in place, one should ensure that the battery operated computer has had the same version of the clinic software loaded onto its hard drive as is used on the main clinic computer and that the battery is always fully charged.

The client materials that cannot be electronically recorded are best kept in a clearly labeled manila folder, in a filing cabinet. The filing cabinet should preferably be made of steel and not situated on or near combustible materials, so as to reduce potential damage in the event of a fire.

9. Dispensary Management

For those clinics dispensing medicines, attention needs to be paid to the methods of operating the dispensary, and the ways and means of maximising efficiencies in this area.

Dispensary Records

Careful records should be kept of the details related to the activities in the dispensary, and this is normally done through the use of a batch book. This may be kept on a computer or may take the form of a book into which one enters these details by hand. The entries should cover all of the aspects of dispensing, and a snap-shot view of a batch book may look like the following.

The Happy Herbalist. Norman Happy DBM. 10 Helianthus Drive Happy Hill Qld 4006 Ph/Fax 07-31190004 Prov. No. J99904A ABN 99 777 001 555 www.happy.com.au	Dispensary Batch Book		
	Client name	Client name	Client name
Date prescribed			
Herb			
Supplier			
Batch No			
Expiry date			
Quantity supplied			
Herb			
Supplier			
Batch No			
Expiry date			
Quantity supplied			
Herb			
Supplier			
Batch No			
Expiry date			
Quantity supplied			
Total volume of herbs supplied			
Dose			

The same method of entry should be used for every single product dispensed and given to clients, including homoeopathic medicines.

It's important to record all of these details. In the event of a product recall or a client experiencing an adverse reaction, it's essential to know exactly what was given to each client and it's essential to be able to trace an ingredient back to the supplier. Without the capacity to do this, in the event of client experiencing a serious adverse reaction, and the client taking legal action against the practitioner for damages, the practitioner has nowhere to turn. The ability to provide evidence that the supplier rather than the practitioner was at fault, or the ability to join the supplier in liability is removed unless one can show evidence of the specific details of what was supplied to the client. A copy of these records should be kept off-site so that in the event of a fire or the theft of a computer that may be used to hold the records, a copy of the records remain intact.

Stock Control
One third to one half of a clinics assets may be tied up in dispensary stock. While stock is a significant generator of profit it can also be a drain on resources if it's not properly managed- stock sitting on shelves should be thought of as money sitting on shelves. Controlling stock levels is essential because excessive stock holding ties up working capital. Stock has a fixed shelf life, and the longer it is kept, the more it is likely to expire before it's sold.

Therefore, one should attempt to minimise the time that stock is held in the dispensary, and buying smaller quantities more frequently rather than buying larger quantities less frequently minimises the risk of having capital lying dormant on stock shelves.

For example, the typical natural therapies clinic may, at any one time, be holding the following stock:

Stock	Units held	Weeks worth of stock	Wholesale cost $
Slow moving herbs- 2 of each	60x500mL	4	2100
Fast moving herbs- 4 of each	100x500mL	4	3500
Slow moving supplements- 4 of each	40	4	440
Fast moving supplements- 6 of each	120	4	1320
Homoeopathics- 1 of each	150x50mL	8	1667
10mL Bottles and drip. caps	250	8	100
200mL bottles and caps	250	8	96
Total cost			$9223

One should only keep enough stock on hand to cover 2 delivery periods. If for example, the normal time period taken to have stock delivered to the clinic from the time of order was 1 week and delivery was free, then only enough stock should be kept on hand to cover 2 weeks trading. This allows for any delivery problems that may delay the arrival of stock. If there were a charge on delivering orders under a $300 wholesale value of $15 and 2 weeks stock only amounted to a value of $100, then it may be worth ordering another weeks stock to take advantage of the free delivery, but such a practice often represents false economy.

If the levels of stock from the example above were reduced to cover 2 weeks of trading where feasible rather than the 4 to 8 seen above, the stock holding may look like the following.

Stock	Units held	Weeks worth of stock	Wholesale cost $
Slow moving herbs- 1 of each	30x500mL	2	1050
Fast moving herbs- 2 of each	45x500mL	2	1750
Slow moving supplements- 2 of each	20	2	220
Fast moving supplements- 3 of each	60	2	660
Homoeopathics- 1 of each*	150x50mL	8	1667
10mL Bottles and drip. caps**	125	4	50
200mL bottles and caps**	125	4	48
Total cost			**$5445**

*The nature of homoeopathic single remedies is such that one may not easily predict what will be needed in the immediate future, so minimising stock levels on the basis of perceived future requirements is not feasible for these products.
**Bottles, caps and inserts are normally sold in packs such as 125, and buying parts of a pack frequently involves cost penalties. Given the cost of these materials, holding extra stock is not a critical issue.

From the example above it can be seen that rationalising stock holdings can liberate a significant amount of capital that would otherwise be totally inactive. This example showed a cost saving of $3778. If, for instance, the savings made above were to be spent on radio advertising that cost $50 per 15 second ad, and each ad on average produced 3 new clients, this saving could bring 227 new clients into the practice. If each new client represented an average income of $75, without consideration to follow up consultations, this investment could generate an increase in income of $17,025. By buying less more frequently, one may miss out on bulk buy discounts or free freight that may be offered by some wholesalers, but these are greatly outweighed by the potential inherent in the savings gained by reduced stock holding.

The Business of Healing

Ordering Stock

Firstly, it's advantageous to confine your trading to one wholesaler rather than five manufacturers. One cheque sent out to pay for stock every month instead of five cheques can save a great deal of paperwork. In most states, suppliers exist that carry the major brands of prescribed natural products. Organisations such Lifespan in Queensland, New South Wales and Victoria, Waiva Clark in Queensland, Traditional Medicine Supplies in New South Wales, Obourne Health Supplies in Victoria, Betta Life in South Australia, and Renner Health Supplies in Western Australia all stock most brands of these products. These organisations frequently run discounts on specific stock lines, arrange seminars and produce newsletters advertising new products. They may also provide discounts for early payment or regular high turnover, and their wholesale prices are generally the same as the price charged by the manufacturer. When opening an account with a manufacturer or wholesaler, one will normally have to fill out a credit application and will be given a copy of the company's trading terms. Careful attention should be paid to these trading terms, note taken of the conditions under which one will be purchasing goods, and the penalties or situations that may arise if one does not pay for stock within a certain period of time.

Ensure also that the supplier you use can deliver stock overnight in you need something urgently- there'll normally be an extra charge for this, and it's wise to have access to a second supplier if any problems arise with your primary wholesaler.

Ordering stock is best done by fax or e-mail, and if by fax it's best done on the wholesalers own fax order form (ask for these from the wholesaler). Many more mistakes are made with telephone orders than with faxed or e-mailed orders, these latter save confusion at the wholesalers end, and you have a record or what was ordered and when.

One should never accept stock that is close to its expiry date, or any stock that is damaged. These should be reported to the supplier within 24 hours and the stock replaced by the supplier. When receiving goods from suppliers, one should carefully inspect the order and ensure that it contains no broken items, what has arrived is what was ordered, and that none of the items are near their expiry dates.

Stocktaking

The practitioner or more commonly the receptionist should keep a running record of stock sold so that the person ordering stock knows when the re-order point has arrived. These records should state the individual products, how many are in stock, and the wholesale value of the current stock levels. Full stocktakes of all of the products should be done every 6 months by the person who normally orders stock and this should be checked against the running record to ensure that these figures are accurate. The records should also detail who performed the stocktake and when it was done. These figures should be monitored to ensure that the value of dispensary stock is kept to a minimum, and a copy of the stock records should be kept off-site so that in the event of a fire or burglary, detailed claims can be made on one's insurance. Stock values should be at current replacement value. Stock records are best kept on a computer using dedicated stock surveillance software which can be fairly easily obtained from most computer software suppliers.

Dispensing Medicines

One should ensure that products are correctly labelled as previously mentioned, the labels are secure and the printing on the label is not water-soluble. Pre-printed labels can be obtained from printers, or blank labels may be stamped with the appropriate details and stamps obtained from local stamp suppliers, or computer software such as "Labelmaker" used to print labels. It's also useful to tell the client what they are being given and how to take it and repeat the dose instructions on client advice sheets, given to the client at the end of the consultation or when at reception after the consultation.

Pricing

Dispensed items should be priced at a certain percentage above the wholesale price- a 50-80% markup is the norm, although this is largely a matter of personal choice. If the stock one supplies is also available from nearby retail outlets, one should be aware of the prices they charge for these items, and not stray too far from them. One may also wish to consider not carrying these products and sending the client to the retailer with a request that they purchase them there. This can reduce the apparent cost of the treatment and encourages client referrals from those retailers.

Miscellaneous Issues

One should avoid using stock that is out of date- expiry may make the goods technically defective and supplying those goods may be in breach of the Trade Practices Act. This situation is the same for any damaged goods. Expired stock should be discarded.

Keeping a separate bank account for sales of dispensary goods, and using this account only for the purchase of dispensary stock, ensures that one will always have enough money to purchase stock.

By positioning the oldest stock at the front of the dispensary shelves, one is always assured of using this stock first., and it can save a great deal of time if the more frequently used items are placed within the easiest reach.

10. Employing Staff

Anyone taking a professional and serious approach to their practice should employ a receptionist. The principal advantages in doing so lay in the areas of efficiency of the operation of the clinic, professionalism in regard to client booking and reception activities, and again, being able to separate the commercial relationship with the client from the therapeutic relationship. These advantages cannot necessarily be quantified from a financial perspective, but in the long term the benefits definitely outweigh the costs. Whilst it's desirable to be able to employ a receptionist, one still needs to be able to fund the position, therefore the first consideration should be whether or not the cash flow will allow for the payment of a receptionist. To this end, one should be aware of the total cost and the various activities that need to be performed to allow this to happen. These issues will be discussed later.

Job Descriptions

The next consideration should be the job description. This outlines the position description, the duties inherent in the position as well as the skills, experience and aptitudes required for the job. A job description may look something like this:

The Happy Herbalist Norman Happy DBM. 10 Helianthus Drive Happy Hill Qld 4006 Ph/Fax 07-31190004 Prov. No. J99904A ABN 99 777 001 555 www.happy.com.au	Job Description Form

Position description:
        Receptionist
Classification:
        Full time	

Experience Required:
        General reception duties- at least 5 years
        Word processing
        Cash handling and reconciliation
        General bookkeeping
        Stock control
        Marketing	

Preferred Personality Profile:
        Positive
        Outgoing
        Efficient
        Professional
        Committed to the success of the practice	

	Loyal
	Punctual
	Honest
	Accurate
	Enthusiastic
	Compassionate
	The ability to prioritise tasks
	Industrious
	Self motivated
	Proactive
	Autonomous
	Excellent communicator
Duties:	
	Managing and maintaining reception area
	Answering the telephone
	Converting telephone enquiries to appointment bookings
	Taking appointment bookings
	Confirming bookings
	Client file management
	Receipt and cash management
	Bookkeeping
	Ordering therapeutic goods
	Stock control
	Construction of marketing material
Appearance:	
	Neat professional
Classification	
	Full time permanent
Date........................	
Receptionist.................................	
Employer..	

As with all forms used within the clinic, the form should be headed with the clinic details and the type of form stated. The position and classification is defined, and the experience necessary to perform the job is also clearly defined. With this and subsequent categories, the competencies and qualities outlined may be preferred rather than mandatory for the position.

Consideration should be given to the hours you'd like a receptionist to work. This may be full time for preference, i.e. whenever the clinic is operating, but the funds may only allow for a part-time position, in which case the receptionist should be operating during the clinics' busiest periods, for example, Monday, Tuesday, Thursday and Friday. It may also be appropriate to hire a receptionist to work the busier hours of the say, from 10 am to 3 p.m. for example. For the purposes of defining the terms, full time is 38 hours per week, part time means regular hours less than 38 hours but more than 12 hours per week. Casual refers to hours worked as less than 38 hours per week but those hours are worked at irregular periods.

The section headed Experience Required outlines the successful applicants preferred background. If that person has an excellent personality and is deficient in experience, various government departments may be able to provide subsidies for training. The state Departments of Small Business and the federal Department of Industry and Trade, mentioned in the Resources section, can advise on this issue.

The Preferred Personality Profile may seem like an impossible blend of attributes to find in one person but these are the attributes one should be looking for in a receptionist. The person you hire to fill this position is the first person to come in contact with potential or existing clients, and as such, skills in the areas of interpersonal relations must be excellent and the person should reflect what you and your clinic stand for. The salient characteristic here is attitude. A clinic may possibly survive with a practitioner with a less than perfect attitude, but no clinic can survive with a receptionist with a poor attitude. This individual must also be committed to the success of the practice to the same degree as the practitioner if not more so. It's also useful to remember that the employer will be responsible for the actions of employees under the Vicarious Liability rule mentioned earlier.

The nature of the business requires that the receptionist will be acting alone and unsupervised for much of the time, and this will require a high level of commitment, motivation, enthusiasm and efficiency to competently manage the many and varied tasks inherent in the role. The variety of tasks involved in the job will demand an ability to prioritise those tasks, recognising that the needs of the client are paramount. A high degree of honesty and integrity will also be required due to the temptations that a continuous cash flow may provide to some people. In a solo practice much of the work related to the production of promotional material will also fall on the shoulders of the receptionist.

The section headed, Duties, covers the principal tasks that are required to be carried out by the receptionist and should leave no room for doubt or ambiguity about the job itself. It may seem superfluous to mention dress requirements, but people unaccustomed to the activities of a non-medical healthcare practice may have the impression that tie-dyed clothing and grass sandals are the preferred mode of dress in such an establishment.

Note that cleaning does not appear on the list of duties. Minor tidying may be acceptable, but it has been found that receptionists who are compelled to clean the clinic, on top of all of their other responsibilities, quickly begin to lose their enthusiasm.

Copies of the job description dated and should be signed by the employer and the receptionist and copies held by both parties, so that the potential for disputes about the nature of the job is reduced. As a final point, the word receptionist should not necessarily imply female. There are a number of clinics around the country that operate very effectively with male receptionists.

Recruiting Staff
There are several methods of finding the right person for the job.

The first and most commonly used method of staff acquisition is via the employment section in the local or capital city newspapers. The position may also be listed with the Commonwealth Employment Service (CES) using the Job Network system (see the Australian Government Business Entry Point in the resources section for more on this). You may also wish to enlist the services of an employment agency, and these may be found in the Yellow Pages telephone directory under the heading, Employment Services.

For the purposes of a newspaper or CES advertisement, an advertisement should be constructed. When doing this, note that one cannot discriminate against any applicant on the basis of race, creed, colour, religion or disability. It's useful to ask for references, preferably those who can be contacted by telephone, stipulate whether you want the application to be made in writing or over the phone (for the purposes of hiring someone as a receptionist, this can be constructive), and insert a closing date for applications.

For such an important position as this, once the applications start to come in, it's advisable to perform at least two interviews with the prospective receptionists and you may wish to limit the applicants interviewed to somewhere around ten of the most suitable people. The first interview should be used to check the persons' suitability for the job, and to let them know about hours, duties, salary details, superannuation, holidays, dismissal conditions etc. If the first interview is successful, the second interview should be used to check the persons' suitability to you. One of the advantages of using an employment agency is that much of the work that would normally be done in the first interview can be done by the agency.

Once the candidates have been ranked for suitability, one should select the top three, ask the best of those three if they would like the job (and give them enough time to respond) but keep the other two in mind if the first choice decides not to take up your offer. It can be useful to run a medical check on the person you choose for the job, as the later discovery that this person has some serious or chronic disease can save a great deal of inconvenience and cost. A medical check will often also be necessary for key-person insurance. You may wish to consider the remaining people from the top three as temporary receptionists if an emergency arises. All unsuccessful candidates should be notified that they were not selected, and thanked for their time. When the person starts work you should set aside adequate time for orientation, explanation of facilities, breaks, policies and procedures etc.

As a word of warning in regard to hiring staff, it has been the experience of several practitioners that the hiring of friends, relatives or would-be practitioners, can generate problems. Friendships and relationships with relatives can suffer if a situation arises where one needs to assert one's authority, and would-be practitioners may be tempted to practice their diagnostic and prescribing skills on clients in the waiting room, thereby undermining the future relationship with the practitioner.

Finally on this issue, again, anyone contemplating employing staff should contact Job Network. Contact details are available from your local White Pages telephone directory for details, or use the contact details listed in the Federal section of the Resources chapter in this book. Under the New Enterprise Initiative Scheme (NEIS), which is operated by Job Network centres, certain incentives may be available if one is hiring staff. Additional assistance may be available from the Federal Dept of Employment, Workplace Relations and Small Business.

Employment Contracts

These documents serve a number of very useful functions. They allow the employee to clearly understand what's involved in the job and act as a similar reminder for the employer. They serve as a useful reference in the midst of any dispute about what's involved in the job. They act as a means of instituting methods of measuring success (has the person met or exceeded your expectations as outlined in the contract?), which can be rewarded in an appropriate manner. Normally, both parties sign off on the contract, thereby confirming the responsibilities of each party.

The types of things which should be stipulated in the employment contract are:
- The responsibilities of the employer towards the employee.
- Salary and how it is paid.
- Job classification (part time, full time etc) and grade (clerical grade 1 etc).
- Working conditions.
- Hours of work.
- WorkCover.
- Superannuation.
- Training and regular training review.
- Leave and leave conditions.

- Commencement date.
- Qualifications/competencies and experience required for the job.
- Duties.
- Hours of work, lunch breaks etc.
- Termination details.
- Redundancy agreements.
- Review schedule (how frequently the position is reviewed- this would normally be 3 monthly for the first 6 months in a position such as this and then annually).
- Dismissal details and terms of resignation.

The contract should be signed and dated by both parties and copies held by both the employee and the employer. In regard to the review schedule, this relates to the issue of monitoring performance. To this end, it's useful for both parties to conduct a salary linked performance review every 12 months as a means of discussing performance, and rewarding excellent performance accordingly. The factors that should form part of this review are:

- General job satisfaction.
- Areas for improvement from both sides.
- Employee productivity (for example).
  - The number of telephone calls that the receptionist has converted into bookings.
  - Any innovative ideas that the receptionist has generated that have had a positive effect on the business.
  - The number of mistakes that have been made with booking clients, or any other areas related to the job (best practice should be less than 5%).
- Training audit and discuss areas where training or retraining is required.

Minutes should be taken of the points discussed and any actions that arise from them, and agreement should be given that these actions will be carried out. If there are any areas where the standard is less than satisfactory, it's more constructive to allow the employee to come up with their own means of improving the situation, rather than imposing one upon them. The first two 3 monthly reviews are suggested for the purposes of checking that the job is being properly performed, and both parties are happy with each other.

Responsibilities of the Employer
Employer Registration
If you employ a receptionist or any other person, you then become an employer, and as such there are a number of things that you need to be aware of. Firstly, you'll need to register as an employer. This is done through an application for registration as a group employer from the Instalments Section of the ATO. Contact the ATO for more on this.

Employment Records
Records of employment need to be kept, and these consist of:
- The name of employee.
- The name of employer.
- The date that employment was commenced.
- Classification (full, or part time permanent, temporary or casual).
- Grading (clerical grade 1 to 5).
- Hours worked.
- Remuneration rate, how this is paid and how frequently (this is normally every 2 weeks).
- Gross salary and any deductions.
- Leave entitlements.
- Leave taken by the employee.
- Leave accrued.
- Superannuation contributions, the period over which these have been made, when they are made and the name of superannuation fund.
- Union membership and any disciplinary actions taken.
- Any enterprise bargaining arrangements that have been made.
- Termination date if the employment has been terminated.

The records must be made available to the employee on demand and if the business changes hands the old employer must keep a copy of the records. The records may be inspected by officers of the Department of Industrial Relations at any time. These records need to be kept on the premises for at least 6 years.

Payment
In regard to the payment of salary, the method of payment should be determined by the employee (unless stipulated by the appropriate award), and the payment needs to be accompanied by a payment advice slip. This slip should state:
- The names of the employee and employer.
- The classification of the employee.
- Payment date.
- Period of employment for which the payment applies.
- The gross amount of payment.
- Annual and long service leave entitlements, overtime etc (separately identified).
- The amount deducted for tax.
- Superannuation and any other payments made on behalf of the employee.
- The net amount paid.

Awards
The payment of salaries and wages to most sections of the workforce is covered by awards. These outline the pay and conditions pertinent to the jobs and various grades covered by the award. Receptionists are covered by clerical awards, within

which 5 grades exist, and there are different rates of pay for each grade and each classification (full time, part time and casual).

As an example, the adult full time award for a Grade 1 clerical worker in NSW is $424.60 per week, rising to $577.50 per week for Grade 5. The award for a part time adult in NSW is $11.18 per hour for Grade 1 to $15.20 for Grade 5. The casual rate per hour is the same as the part time rate plus an additional 20%. Lower rates exist for juniors (under 21), these being (in NSW) $212 per week for a full time 17 year old, $261 per week at 18, $298 at 19 and $352 at 20. Working on a Saturday normally attracts a loading, and in NSW, the rate of pay is 1.5 times the normal hourly rate, for all grades and ages, apart from casuals. Awards may vary from state to state and may change from time to time. Wageline and the various state employment departments can supply information on awards.

Enterprise Bargaining Agreements
These are employment agreements made between the employer and the employee setting out the rights and responsibilities of each party. These agreements may be perpetual or persist for a fixed period and may override any inconsistent award provisions, although they must still comply with state and federal employment legislation. Agreements must not be made that are detrimental to the employee, and if the agreement is made without the involvement of the relevant union, it must be ratified by the Industrial Relations Commission which will determine its suitability. For more on this, contact the Dept of Employment, Workplace Relations and Small Business.

Income Tax
As an employer, you must deduct tax from an employees salary. To organise this, you need to register as an employer with the ATO, which will send you a booklet outlining the method of operation. The amount of tax that needs to be paid can be determined from the taxation schedules available from the ATO or the local post office. As a part of these arrangements you'll need to ask your employee to fill out an employment declaration form (available from the ATO) and send this back to the ATO (keeping a copy for the employees' record). If declaration forms are not sent in, the ATO will assume that the employee is to pay the maximum tax rate. There is also a requirement to supply the employee with a group certificate by July 14 of each year, listing all salary and deductions for the previous financial year, and a copy needs to be sent to the ATO by August 14 of that year.

Fringe Benefits Tax
This relates to any non-monetary benefit provided to an employee. This benefit is subject to taxation that may be paid at a rate different to that listed on the standard tax schedule. Contact the ATO for more on this.

Medicare Levy
As a means of covering the costs of providing public healthcare, the federal government imposes a levy on the salary of all employees. This is payable to Medicare at a rate of 1.5% of the employees gross salary, and the levy increases to 2.5% for employees whose gross salary is in excess of $50,000 per year. Contact the various state departments of health or the ATO for more on this.

Superannuation
As a means of providing an income for employees after retirement, it's a requirement that superannuation payments be made on behalf of employees. This is not required if the employee is under 18 or over 70 years of age, if employed for less then 30 hours per week, or if the employee is paid less than $450/month. Employees may have to have been employed for 3 months before superannuation contributions need to be made.

Superannuation payments are made by lodging 9% of the employees gross salary with a complying superannuation fund or retirement savings account. To check which funds comply, contact the Australian Prudential Regulatory Authority on 1300 131060. Payments are normally made monthly and must be accompanied by the employee's tax file number, the employers tax file number, the employers and employees address details, the payment amount, and the period to which the payment applies. For more on this, contact the Superannuation Guarantee Coordinator at the ATO. Superannuation contribution records must be kept for at least 5 years.

WorkCover
As a means of meeting the medical costs of employees injured whilst at work, it's a requirement that an amount of 1.41% of an employees gross salary (including superannuation) be paid to the WorkCover Authority. To arrange this, register with the WorkCover Authority within 14 days of employing staff. For more on this, contact the WorkCover Corporation.

Occupational Health and Safety
It is a requirement under the Occupational Health, Safety and Welfare Act that employers:
• Provide a safe working environment.
• Develop and provide safe systems of work.
• Consult with employees on changes to the workplace and the management of workplace hazards.
• Provide adequate facilities for the welfare of employees.
• Provide information, instruction and training in any area that could involve hazards.
• Provide adequate supervision to ensure employees are safe from hazards and disease.

- Monitor employees health and welfare.
- Keep records of injuries.
- Monitor working conditions.

A breach of any one of these issues may render an employer liable to prosecution under the terms of the Act. Policies and procedures should be developed to ensure that problems in this area don't arise, and employees should be actively involved in the construction of these policies and procedures.

Unions

An employee has the right to join a union if they wish. One of the implications of this is that an officer or an employee of a union to which an employee belongs has the right to enter the business premises for the purpose of inspecting employee records, without the employers' consent, after they've obtained permission to do so from the Industrial Relations Commission.

Leave Entitlements

An integral part of employing staff is making allowances for leave. There are several different facets to this.

Long Service Leave

Long service leave is available to all full time, part time and casual employees, on a pro rata basis. A person working full time with the same employer for an unbroken period of 10 years (note that parental leave doesn't constitute a break in service) is entitled to 2 months paid leave, and 1 month for every 5 years thereafter. A person is also entitled to long service leave on a pro rata basis after 5 years if they resign as a result of illness, incapacity, domestic or other pressing necessity or are dismissed for any reason other than serious or wilful misconduct. Long service leave cannot be paid out, and an employee taking long service leave has the right to ask for and receive the payment for this period in advance, or may elect to take it in normal instalments. One thing to bear in mind here is that the employer is the business, not the practitioner. If one purchases an existing practice and anyone employed by the business stays on, the accrual of long service as well as all other forms of leave is continuous through the change of ownership.

Annual Leave

Annual leave is available to all full and part-time workers, and may be available to casual staff after a fixed period of employment. It normally consists of 20 paid days per year, taken at a time agreed to by both the employer and the employee. Leave is normally not able to be taken until the anniversary of the first day of employment and after that it can be taken within 6 months of the due date. Any unused annual leave must be paid out when an employee leaves their employment.

Sick Leave

Sick leave also needs to be available to full time and part time employees, and may also be available to casual employees after a fixed period of employment has elapsed. Accrual of sick leave may or may not be done at employers discretion and it normally consists of 10 paid days per year.

Parental Leave

Parental leave is another form of leave entitlement available to full and part time employees, and casual staff after a certain time. The leave is unpaid, it can be taken for maternal leave in connection with pregnancy or birth (for up to 52 weeks), it can be taken as paternal leave for birth (up to 1 week or by agreement), or up to 3 weeks leave can be taken as adoption leave in connection with the adoption of a child under 5 years or age. In many circumstances an employee will be asked to provide a statutory declaration stating the facts regarding this leave before it may be granted. An employee cannot be dismissed while on this leave, and if the working conditions are deemed to be unsafe or the hours of work unsuitable for the pregnant employee, the employer must make the necessary changes in the workplace.

Dismissal

A situation may arise where consideration needs to be given to the dismissal of an employee. Hopefully this situation never occurs, but if it does it's well to be prepared for it. In the event of an employee acting in a manner that's detrimental to the business, unless the action involves a serious issue (theft etc), the person needs to be given three warnings in writing in regard to these actions before they can be dismissed.

The dismissed person has the right to sue the employer under the unfair dismissal legislation, through the Industrial Affairs Commission. The person needs to apply to the Commission for the matter to be heard, after which the Commission will make a decision and recommend an appropriate course of action. One of the aims of defining the reasons for dismissal in an employees employment contract is to minimise problems that may arise in these kinds of areas. For more on this contact the Dept of Employment, Workplace Relations and Small Business or Wageline.

Managing Staff Shortages

Staff shortages may arise if the practitioner, receptionist or other staff member is unable to attend the practice. As mentioned earlier, it's wise to make provisions in your policies and procedures manual for the use of a locum in the event that one is unfit for work. It's also useful to have a contract with the nominated locum that prohibits this person from poaching your clients- your clients need to stay with your clinic, not transfer their needs to the clinic normally occupied by the locum.

If you employ a receptionist you may either wish to consider having an arrangement with one or both of the other top three applicants for the original receptionists position, or you may wish to contact local employment agencies with a view to being able to access a temporary receptionist (preferably a medical receptionist) in the event that the receptionist is unfit for work. If the latter occurs, the temporary receptionist should be given adequate orientation and guidance, she or he should carefully briefed on what you do and asked to study the policies and procedures manual.

11. Marketing

The primary function of marketing is communication, the aim of which is to attract new business to the clinic through advertising and promotional activities. It's essentially about transmitting what you want to say, using methods that will get to the people you want to get to in a way that they can understand and remember. Successful marketing relies upon sound research on the market, understanding that market, and constructing and transmitting a marketing message using the appropriate marketing tools. Monitoring the results of this activity will then assist in determining any changes that might be required.

Since the main aim of marketing is to increase one's business activity, it will be of most use in the first few years after the practice is established, and become somewhat less important as things such as referrals from present and past clients, and the Yellow Pages, dominate as referral sources. However, a certain amount of marketing should be maintained if one wishes the practice to grow.

Whilst marketing is very important to the success of one's business, one's enthusiasm for it should be tempered by the fact that it costs seven times more to attract new clients into one's practice than it does to retain an existing client. Therefore, while marketing is important, one's focus on it should never take priority over the means by which one retains the current clients.

Market Research- Understanding the Market

For your marketing messages to be effective there needs to be a sufficient number of the right type of people within easy reach of the practice, and one needs to understand these people. The 2 main areas of market research that apply to the industry are a definition of the marketing area, and a demographic analysis to better understand how best to communicate with potential clients.

The Marketing Area

Otherwise known as the target area, this is the geographically defined area within which one will carry out the marketing activities. How many of the people in this area one is likely to have access to can be roughly determined by their ability and willingness to get to you. It's also affected by whether one operates a general practice, or specialises in a particular area.

It should be kept in mind that while one can't be all things to all people, those who specialise and therefore rely on one narrowly defined market segment do so at their peril. Fluctuations that occur in the market place do so with much more vigor in narrowly defined markets than those where the broader community are targeted, and these fluctuations can have a significant impact on one's business.

In metropolitan areas where people use motor vehicles as their main mode of transport, the area from which one will be drawing clients is roughly bounded by the distance it takes to drive for twenty minutes in any direction away from the clinic. For the average person seeking the services of a non-medical healthcare provider, having to travel for more than twenty minutes is often seen as an inconvenience. If one were to drive for twenty minutes in a direction north from the clinic, north east from the clinic, and so on around all of the points of the compass, and make a mark on a local map where one stopped and joined the dots, the area within this circle is roughly the area from which one will be drawing clients. If one specialises in treating a particular condition or works with one particular client group, the acceptable travel time may be increased.

This twenty minute distance will also be greater in rural areas, where most people are used to having to drive longer distances, and will be increased in metropolitan areas when one is situated close to some other point of attraction, such as a major shopping centre. The distance may also slightly increase if one is located near a major road. Older and retired people may also tolerate a longer period of travel. Public transport access may also increase this area, as most people are generally happy to spend slightly longer in public transport than they are negotiating the roads. This defined area, given that it contains enough of the right type of people, will become the marketing area.

Unless one specialises in paediatric care, geriatric care, or the care of any other specific group in the community, research (MacLennan AH, et al, Prevalence and Cost of Alternative Medicine in Australia, Lancet, 347, March 2, 1996, 569-573) indicates that the main group or demographic that uses natural and complementary therapies are well educated, single, employed, middle class women aged roughly between 15 and 34. These are the people to whom the marketing should be directed or targeted. If the marketing area doesn't contain any of them, then the marketing will be wasted. If they're concentrated in a small area, marketing activities can be concentrated on this one area.

If, using local census data, one found that 20% of the population within the 20 minute radius consisted of the demographic described above, and the total population within this area was 50,000, then it is conceivable, depending upon the level of real competition and the populations' level of disposable income, that one is working with a potential client base of 10,000 people. If the demographic are in short supply within the marketing area, then the decision should be made to either expand the marketing area to reach enough of them to make the practice viable, or move the location of the practice to a more suitable area.

Local census data, derived from the ABS (Australian Bureau of Statistics) can be useful in analysing the target area. This data is taken from the national census, which is carried out once every four years, and is usually available for local council areas. The data fields it generates outline local, state and national area details on age, background, language spoken, employment status, housing status, family type (couple or single parent), number of children and their ages. Level of income, whether the dwelling occupied is owned or rented, numbers of those working and unemployed, working full time, part time or casual, type of work done, education background and a great deal more information can be garnered from these resources.

Demographic Analysis

Demography is the science of vital and social statistics. A demographic analysis is used to aid in understanding some of the key factors that relate to the market and the people that we aim to communicate with. This understanding will assist in forming decisions related to the methods that will be used in advertising. Factors that need to be considered are:

- *Who we need to talk to.* What sort of person is the most likely to want to use our services? Who are our services most likely to benefit? Again, this will be influenced by whether one operates a general or specialised practice. For example, those specialising in peadiatrics will need to be able to talk to the parents or carers of young children, and access to school teachers and the operators of day care centres will also be useful.
- *What we want to say to them?* We need to find out what it is that we have that they can use. It's not enough for an osteopath to say that he or she practices osteopathy and hopes that the population understands the implications of this. One needs to understand the predominant health problems and fears of the community, and express the benefits of osteopathy in these terms. It may be that the local community consists mainly of manual labourers, many of whom fear the effect that musculoskeletal disorders may have on their ability to earn a living. Rather than state that one is an osteopath, a more appealing message will link the benefits of osteopathy with these fears. Reliable information on what the needs and fears of the community may be can be had from health food stores, pharmacies, and other practitioners in the local area as well as newspapers and other local media.
- *How we can reach them?* Where does our typical client live? What newspapers or magazines do they read? Which radio station do they listen to? What types of media (print, radio, television, direct mail etc) are they likely to notice? For

the practitioner specialising in geriatric healthcare, little will be gained from leaving brochures at the local gymnasium and paying for advertising on a hard rock radio station. The marketing message needs to be transmitted at a time and place that will be noticed by the demographic and designed in a manner that will attract, appeal, and generate a desire to contact you.

The demographic analysis will be looked at in more detail later in the section headed Marketing Plan.

The Marketing Message

One of the keys to successful marketing is knowing what to say and how to say it. Once one has discovered the needs of the community, it becomes easier to know what to say. If, for example, the majority of the community are routinely using some form of pharmaceutical product, and the local media reflect concerns regarding the level of side effects of this product, the local homoeopath would do well to use the safety of homoeopathy as an integral part of the marketing message. The message should also imply (without breaching any relevant legislation) that through his or her training, skills and experience in dealing with the issue, the practitioner is the one best placed to deal with the issue at hand. This is otherwise known as selling the competitive advantages of the practitioner and it's largely reliant upon perception.

Competitive Advantage

We may have the same skills and aptitudes as the next person practicing our modality, but the way the community perceives the marketing message that we send out may elevate our attraction to a level well above the other practitioner. The perception of the message will be reinforced by the image we present- the clothes we wear, the vehicle we drive, the type of language we use, the way the clinic is presented, the type of stationary used and everything about us. All of these things can be and are used by successful marketers to reinforce their central marketing message.

Further to the issue of the competitive advantage, this should be assessed on the community's criteria rather than our own. For example we may perceive our competitive edge to be the fact that we have the highest level of training in our particular modality in the community. This may mean nothing to the local community. It may be that the issue of easy parking is of much greater importance to the target market, and if one's clinic did in fact excel in this area, this should become one of the main competitive advantages and form a key part of the marketing message. It can be an interesting exercise to discover the needs and priorities of the local community and these issues should be kept clearly in mind when thinking about competitive advantages and constructing the marketing message.

Constructing the Message
The marketing message should not necessarily be centred around a fixed issue. One may have a core message that is regularly transmitted, perhaps incorporating one's primary competitive advantages and slogan, and one may also wish to transmit messages of a more seasonal or reactive nature. For example, if one has skills in dealing with hay fever, material advertising this fact should only be transmitted immediately prior to and during the hay fever season. If one has skills in dealing with a transient condition, for example a transient outbreak of gastroenteritis, this also should be transmitted whilst the condition is present, beginning as close as possible to the beginning of the outbreak.

In general, the message itself needs to be able to do 4 things:
- *Get the persons attention-* this can be done in a variety of ways. One may use eye-catching headers, one may choose a unique venue (skywriting for example- expensive but novel on a calm day), one may use unique colours or typefaces etc as a means of getting attention. One thing to keep in mind here is that the average city dweller will see or hear somewhere between two and five thousand marketing message per day. Unless one's message is novel or unique in some way, it will be invisible amongst the backdrop of all of the other messages that are clamouring for attention.
- *Appeal to their needs-* market research will reveal what these needs are, and one needs to encapsulate these clearly and succinctly.
- *Offer an attractive solution to those needs-* clearly and succinctly transmit the notion that you have the solution to the problem. This solution needs to be offered in a way that the intended recipient can understand. The solution needs to be just that- a clearly identifiable solution. To take an example from hardware retailing, if one sells electric drills- the marketer doesn't sell the drill, he or she sells the hole that the purchaser will be making with the drill. The hole is the solution, the drill is simply the means by which one gets to it. American advertising analysts have found that most buyers of products or services in the USA do so for one of three reasons- fear (of disease, loss etc), need (for survival etc) or greed, and these factors should be borne in mind. It's also important here to highlight one's competitive advantages.
- *Provide a means of contact-* this will be somewhat dependent on your demographic and how they normally communicate- commonly this will be by telephone, but may also be by e-mail. One should also state the location of the clinic as a means of assisting with the perception that you're close and easy to reach.

Throughout this, the message needs to be set in the language of the intended audience, which is not necessarily the same as the language normally used by the person writing the message. It should also reflect much of the attitude of the intended audience. If that audience is predominantly female, the imagery and text used should be those that will appeal more to women.

The message should be kept simple, using simple language and simple concepts. One should never assume that a clever marketing message is going to be understood by everyone in one's target market. In fact one should be aiming at the lowest level of intelligence within that sector.

One final point on this issue is that whilst one should take a professional approach to marketing, one must be passionate about one's business and the marketing of it if it's to succeed. A lack of passion on the part of the marketer will translate to a low level of motivation by the target market and a poor response to the marketing.

Transmitting the Message
How, when, where and how frequently the marketing message is transmitted will have a significant bearing on its effectiveness.

Marketing Media
There is a multitude of means or media by which one can transmit the marketing message. The types of media used may be newspapers, magazines, radio, television, internet web sites, outdoor media such as billboards, taxibacks, bus ads, bus stops, and anything else that provides an effective means of transmitting the message. One may also select a mix of these various media, depending upon which ones are successful.

All of these have various cost implications and one of the best methods of determining which is most appropriate is via a cost versus benefit analysis, or in the case of marketing, cost per impact. The cost per impact is calculated by dividing the cost by the number of people who see it, or per impact. An ad in a local newspaper may cost $50 per week and, using the newspapers own circulation figures, reaches 10,000 households. In this example, if only one person in that household were to read that newspaper, the cost per impact would be half of one cent ($50.00 divided by 10,000). It may cost $170 to have 1000 folded direct mail brochures produced, and another $30 to have them delivered. If only one person in each of the households to which the brochures were delivered were to see them, the cost per impact here would be 20 cents ($200.00 divided by 1000). On a cost per impact basis, the newspaper advertisement looks like a much better investment, but this needs to be weighed against the fact that the newspaper carries many advertisements that are competing for the attention of the reader. The reader may not be the sort of person who would normally seek your services, whereas direct mail brochures may be targeted at areas where there are higher proportions of these people.

Different media also has different characteristics. For example, some people may keep a direct mail brochure for a lot longer than they keep a newspaper, and magazines are kept for longer than newspapers. Depending on where they're located and how the marketing message is conveyed, billboards can attract more attention than an advertisement on the back of a taxi or the side of a bus.

Context also plays a part. The context or environment in which the ad appears will influence who hears or sees it, and we need to know that those listening or looking are our main demographic if the ad is going to be effective. One would get a much greater response by advertising the services of a naturopath during a radio health program than on a radio sporting show, unless of course the naturopath is specialising in sports nutrition, for example.

The media one chooses to use should take cost per impact, the characteristics and the context into consideration, and the media which provides the best option chosen.

Spread
It's important to consider how widely one wants to broadcast the message. Considering the previous discussion on the marketing or target area, it may be that money spent on carrying the message too far out of this area will be wasted because the people it reaches are outside the area where they can conveniently get to you. If, however, your area of expertise is specialised rather than general, the spread should be as wide as possible.

A naturopath specialising in general healthcare should, at least initially, confine her or his marketing activities to the defined target area. A naturopath specialising in fertility management for example will benefit from spreading the marketing message as widely as possible. Given that the demographic, i.e. couples experiencing difficulty with conception, only form a small percentage of the community, for a sufficient number of people to be attracted to the practice the spread needs to be broader than for the practitioner operating a general practice.

Frequency
The frequency with which the message is transmitted is an important consideration. On average, it takes seven repetitions of the same message before it's noticed, and once noticed, three repetitions of the message are required before the message is acted upon. The frequency required may also be influenced by the type of media used, the content of the message, and how many other marketing messages are competing with it for attention.

Direct mail brochures of a general advertising nature should be sent out monthly to reinforce the general advantages of the clinic to the community. Direct mail brochures advertising help for seasonal or transient conditions should be sent out immediately prior to the season and then weekly for seven to ten weeks for seasonal conditions, or should be discontinued before this if the prevalence of the condition diminishes earlier. Direct mail brochures advertising one's services for transient conditions should be sent out as close to the beginning of the appearance of the condition as possible, continued weekly and discontinued as soon as its prevalence begins to wane. Experience has shown that direct mail doesn't necessarily provoke an immediate response- some people hold on to a brochure for months before they act on it.

Local weekly newspaper advertisements should be a relatively permanent fixture, or at the very least placed in the same position in the paper every two weeks.

Because of the sheer information density of a medium such as radio, radio ads should be transmitted half hourly during programs that are likely to have the largest audience of one's demographic. It may be that the local radio station runs a health program between 7 and 9 p.m. every Thursday night, therefore one would buy, for example, four 30 second spots during this time.

Outdoor ads such as those placed on billboards, taxi-backs, bus stop seats and enclosures are normally fixed for the period of time that one pays for.

Advertising Regulations
One needs to be aware of the fact that there are numerous regulations that control the content of advertisements. Of these that apply to the healthcare industry, it is an offence to:
- Falsely represent that goods are of a particular standard, quality or value.
- Falsely claim that goods or services have the sponsorship or endorsement of an individual or organisation.
- Falsely represent the price of goods or services.
- Falsely represent the origin of goods.
- Falsely represent the need for any services or goods.
- Falsely represent any warranty or guarantee relating to goods or services.
- Charge the higher price when more than one price appears on an item held out for sale- the item must be sold for the lowest price shown.

Marketing Media
A number of means exist through which one can transmit one's marketing message. These are generally referred to as marketing or advertising media, consisting of electronic media such as radio and television, print media such as magazines and newspapers, outdoor, direct mail and the internet. Since television is not routinely used to advertise the services of non-medical health clinics, it will not be covered in this discussion.

Radio
Whilst commercial radio can be an advertising dense medium, i.e. carries a large number of ads, the cost per impact can provide excellent value as long as the advertisement used is properly constructed and timed. Like most of the tools

already mentioned, the radio ad should be unique, and contain the four elements mentioned previously:

- Attract attention.
- Appeal to the needs of the audience.
- Offer a solution to those needs.
- Provide a means of contact.

To maximise their impact radio ads should be professionally produced. This can usually be done by the radio station itself, or can be organised through an advertising agency. Careful consideration should be given to when ads are aired, how often they're aired and during which radio program they're aired.

In regard to when they're aired, broadcasting during a health program will maximise the exposure to the main demographic. Taking advantage of the audience increases that occur just prior to hourly news bulletins can also be useful, although the cost per second may be higher during these periods. One should also be aware of when the typical client or demographic is most likely to be listening to the radio.

Cost is also an important consideration. Radio station air time is normally sold by the second, and the cost of airtime may vary from program to program depending on the ratings for that time slot (the higher the ratings, generally the higher the cost), and the period just prior to the news break may attract a higher cost per second. The cost of radio advertising varies between stations and will vary with the day and the time of the day, depending upon the ratings for that period. Rates will also vary somewhat between AM and FM radio. As an example, one 30 second radio ad aired on Sydney AM radio station 2GB between 6 and 8 p.m. on a Saturday night would cost around $150, although the costs usually decrease as one buys more air time. As mentioned above, consideration must be given to the cost per impact.

One should check with the station in question about their ratings- how many are listening and who is listening at what time. The air time purchased should be that during which has the highest numbers of your demographic tuned in.

Radio advertisements can be prepared by advertising agencies for a cost of between $1000 to $5000, and the cost is generally relative to the quality, or if the ad is relatively uncomplicated, it can be recorded by the radio station. The cost of doing this will generally be much less than that done by an agency, but again, the cost may be commensurate with the quality, and can also be affected by the amount of airtime purchased.

The Business of Healing

Radio Interviews
Opportunities exist to be interviewed on radio, either for a fee (paid to the radio station for the opportunity to speak to the stations audience) or for free as a means of creating extra interest in the program. Local commercial radio and particularly local public radio stations will often welcome the opportunity to give some free airtime to healthcare providers. This opportunity is particularly attractive if the speaker has specialist knowledge on a current health topic.

As a means of helping to create this opportunity, approaches should be made to the producer of the program in question, presenting oneself in a professional manner and conveying the offer of an interview. Once the offer has been accepted, there are a number of important issues that need to be considered.

The first of these is that the presenter will often be unfamiliar with your modality and lack the depth of understanding that you may have in the subject proposed for discussion. The presenter will also often be more interested in their own and the stations agenda rather than yours. As such, one needs to develop a short personal biography, a script outlining suggested questions that will maximise the use of the airtime for both you and the station, and ensure that these are used. Your contact details should be mentioned during the interview and reinforced at the end. Allowance may also be made to take questions from listeners.

There are some key elements to successful radio interviews which should be kept in mind. Among these are:
- Speak clearly, distinctly and not too quickly- remember that radio is strictly an audible medium- use as much colour and intonation to your voice as is appropriate- don't speak in a monotone.
- Sound enthused and interested.
- Answers to questions should be brief, concise, complete and avoid jargon- remember who your audience is and what they're capable of grasping.
- Avoid making disparaging remarks regarding colleagues, other professions or other therapeutic products or services if possible- diplomacy should be paramount.
- Keep the microphone positioned slightly below your mouth.
- Work on the assumption that everything that you say is being recorded.
- If you need to cough or clear your throat, most radio studios have a mute button (often marked "cough") somewhere on the desk near to where you're sitting- feel free to use this. Turn away from the microphone to cough if a mute button isn't available.
- Producers and announcers abhor "dead air" or silence during an interview- try to avoid this if possible.
- Consider what you're saying and its' legal ramifications if you're drawn too far from your area of expertise, experience or qualifications.

- If you're being interviewed over the telephone, minimise background noise, and use a landline rather than a mobile telephone if possible.
- Prepare your main marketing message and have it written down in front of you- if necessary, prepare a checklist of things you wish to say, and tick them off as you go.
- Avoid wearing anything that will create background noise (loose jewelry etc).
- Relax- most people prefer to listen to a chat rather than a lecture.
- Stick to your agenda. Accept the presenters lead but don't be driven by it. Listening to politicians answering difficult questions on the radio or television can provide excellent guidance in how to manage the interview.

Scope may also exist to acquire your own health program on a local radio station if the station doesn't operate one already. Some experience in this area and the completion of a panel operators course will be advantageous. A radio station panel operators course may cost somewhere in the region of three to five hundred dollars.

Internet
Australians are great Internet users. Around half of the population use the Internet, and around one third of the population are known to use the Internet to purchase goods or services. The Internet allows a great deal of latitude for the transmission of creative marketing and educational messages.

Through the use of software tools such as Microsoft Netscape Composer, Homepage Maker, Microsoft Frontpage, Macromedia Dreamweaver, and graphics tools such as Adobe Photoshop and Macromedia Fireworks, web sites can be designed that can carry information on the clinic, its functions, location details, consultation costs, information regarding the modalities practiced, and anything else that one wishes to transmit. Webpage creation tips can also be found at http://www.smplanet.com/webpage/webpage.html as well as http://www.netsiteoz.com.au/index.html. This last site also has a domain wizard to assist in registration.

Once the website has been constructed, one can register the domain name with http://www.ina.com.au/register/register.html for a cost of around fifty dollars. This registration provides protection similar to that of a business name. This registration is not mandatory and one may operate a website without registration, but with the accompanying risk. The domain name should be the same as your business name, or should be a name that's derived from it.

The important elements to consider on a webpage or website are those that permeate the rest of this chapter- image, capturing interest, using the language of one's demographic, creating an impulse to contact the clinic, are all essential ingredients. Links can be created to other web sites, and tools such as those found at http://geocities.yahoo.com/v/ao/ptp/ptp sales links.html might be helpful to assist with this activity. The links provided should really only be for services or organisations that support your own activities, and it's useful to regularly ensure that these sites carry links back to your website. In addition, it needs to be kept in mind that the bandwidth of the provider one uses will determine the speed of access to the website- nothing deters Internet surfing more than slow downloads. The maximum amount of storage space available also needs to be considered, as this may determine the how much you can fit onto the website.

The numbers of people accessing the site can be monitored, and entry by registration can be set up to ensure that one has access to the details of those who enter the site.

It should be kept in mind that it's difficult to contain the access to this site to those who reside within the target area. The quality of the site will be proportional to the cost spent on it, or the willingness of Internet-wise friends or relations to contribute time to it.

The services of website designers can be engaged to produce and maintain the site, and while significant costs may be involved in this, specialist attention to this marketing tool can be very beneficial. Designers may also double as webmasters, and it's important to be aware of the ongoing fees charged by webmasters to maintain the site.

It's also important to be aware that unless one registers the site with the main search engines (Altavista, Webcrawler, Anzwers etc), the site will be difficult to access by those who don't know your web site address, and without this registration, those looking for your services, in your area, may not find out that you exist if they use nothing but the Internet. You should also ensure that your website has metatags- words that describe your website and its contents. These enable search engines to find your site and key words in it. To register with the main internet search engines, see http://www.submit-it.com/ or for Australian search engines see either http://websearch.about.com/cs/azsearchengines/ , http://www.adroit.net/support submit oz.html or http://www.geocities.com/SiliconValley/Campus/1282/

Finally, the site should have e-mail capacity to enable electronic contact, and carry all of the normal clinic contact details.

Outdoor
Outdoor advertising consists of things such as signs on the backs of taxis, the backs or sides of buses, signs on bus-stop enclosures and billboards. They can offer good scope for creativity and are mostly visible twenty four hours per day.

In the case of billboards, the advertising costs will be determined largely by their location and because the location is fixed, they can be used in a controlled manner. For example, they can be used in sites such as the sides of main roads that are frequently travelled by the demographic where traffic slows during peak hours, particularly where those roads connect major residential areas with the area where the clinic is located.

The costs of producing outdoor ads can be high, but the cost per impact, if they're properly placed, can be very good. Using Adelaide as an example of the costs of outdoor advertising (excluding production costs), renting space on taxi-backs in Adelaide will cost in the region of $300 per month per taxi, billboards situated in good locations in Adelaide will cost around $150 per week per billboard. Renting space on the back of an Adelaide bus will cost around $380 per bur per month and one 24 foot side panel on a bus may cost around $162 per week. The cost of renting an advertising panel at an Adelaide bus stop will be in the area of $400 per panel for 2 weeks. Prices will differ depending on the city in which the media is located.

Newspapers
Newspapers, particularly local newspapers, offer a relatively cost effective advertising medium and can be fairly well targeted. Costs can also be reduced if one is buying regular advertising space, and the propensity of newspaper editors to allow you free editorial space will be increased by the level of one's advertising expenditure. Unfortunately, the low cost associated with newspaper advertising can attract many other advertisers and it's possible for one's marketing message to be lost in a veritable sea of pleas for investment. As with all marketing tools, careful consideration needs to be given to who one is talking to, what one says, how one says it and how often it's said. It should also be noted that newspaper ads may not reflect as high a level of professionalism as radio or magazine ads.

Again, the ad should attract the readers attention, appeal to their needs, connect with the reader, encourage contact and allow a means for that contact. The contact itself is best done by telephone as this often allows for better initial communication, and for most people, for initial contact it's easier to make a telephone call than it is to travel to the clinic.

For example, a newspaper ad running immediately prior to and during the hay fever season might look like this:

HELP

for hay fever may be closer than you think. See the Happy Herbalist for a natural solution to the sneezing, wheezing and worry of hay fever.
The Happy Herbalist, Happy Hill 07-31190004
Helianthus Drive between the bus depot and Happy Hill public parking station.

As a general rule, the high density level of competing ads means that your ad will require frequent repetition if one wants it to be noticed. It may be appropriate to trial an ad for, say, ten consecutive editions of a weekly newspaper and monitor the results, or run one ad in every second edition of the newspaper. Both methods should be trialed to determine the best use of this medium, and it should be remembered that without repetition, little will be gained from newspaper advertising.

Consideration should be given to where ads appear in a newspaper. The classified ad section is where an ad for a healthcare practice will often be found, but because of the numbers of ads appearing in this area, this is also the best place in which to make it disappear. To increase the visibility and prominence of the ad, it should be placed on one of the right hand pages on one of the top or bottom right hand corners, preferably in the first third of the newspaper. The reasons for the placement are fairly straightforward. When one turns the pages of a newspaper, one usually sees the right hand page first, and the first part of the page one sees, and which therefore the reader has the longest exposure to, is the right hand side of the page. By positioning the ad in either the top or bottom right hand corner, one removes any competing text from two of the four sides of the ad, thereby making the ad more visible. The first third of the newspaper is preferable because the level of the readers interest, and their ability to actually see what they're looking at, wanes as they get further away from the front page.

As a means of confirming the cost per impact figures, most print media such as major newspapers and magazines are audited to determine their readership statistics. As well as the total number of readers, these statistics may cover things such as age range and so on. Local newspapers may only have data on total readership figures.

Magazines Advertisements
At a certain level, magazines may be approached in a similar way to newspapers, although there are some fundamental differences between the two types of media. Magazines are often kept for longer than newspapers, and a magazine is

113

commonly read by a number of people, whereas a newspaper may only be read by one person. Newspapers, particularly the local variants, are generally printed in black and white, whereas the normal preference for a magazine is full colour. This latter feature allows more creativity in the construction of an ad, with an accompanying increase in the potential visibility of the ad. Magazines are seen as a more intimate and personal medium than newspapers and the information contained in them is felt by most to be of high quality. The costs for both production and placement of the ad are higher than those associated with newspapers, and specialist magazines allow one to aim advertising at specific demographic groups.

The readership statistics of magazines are generally better researched and audited than those of local newspapers, so targeting may be somewhat easier, and advance warning by the magazine may be given of the publication of articles that can direct the readers interest to one's ad. For example, an ad for an Osteopathic clinic may be more attractive, and therefore acted upon more rapidly, when placed in a magazine next to an article on back pain, because those reading the article may have an interest in the subject because they suffer from the problem and are seeking solutions to it. The convenient position of the ad, after their interest has been aroused by the article, can expedite contact with the clinic by the reader.

Direct Mail
Direct mail is a useful communication tool and consists of flyers or direct mail letters. It has the advantages of easy targeting, and can be produced and delivered quickly enough to take advantage of new health trends.

Flyers or direct mail brochures are normally cheap, mass produced brochures, often single colour A4 sized paper folded down three ways, and are hand delivered to residential areas one wishes to target. They may be printed in more than one colour, and designed somewhat more exotically than the norm to make them more noticeable and attractive, but the results are not always commensurate with the extra expense involved.

Flyers are particularly useful for sending the community brief and succinct messages about the services that one may be able to provide for the management of seasonal or endemic health problems such as influenza or Ross River fever. They may also be used as a means of introducing oneself to the community when establishing a new business.

One needs to be careful about the targeting of these brochures- and should direct their delivery to areas where the main demographic is known to reside. They should also have the capacity, either through innovative design or some other means, of standing out against what might be a plethora of other direct mail flyers.

The costs involved in direct mail flyers is usually quite small- one can often produce the text and graphics on a personal computer, and have the flyer professionally printed or simply photocopied, although at the volumes usually used, printing is normally cheaper. Printing costs per thousand, using A5 size single sided single brochure printed on normal 90 gram bond paper (the cheapest method available) will cost approximately $30 per thousand. The printing cost per thousand will normally drop as one orders increasingly larger quantities. The more sophisticated the brochure becomes (more colours, better quality paper, double sided etc), the higher the printing costs become. The delivery costs for flyers are minimal- often around $20 to $50 per thousand.

Industry experience has shown that direct mail flyers may be slow to generate a response. It may be that the person receiving the flyer has no reason to act on it at the time that it's received, but will do so should the need arise in the short to medium term. If one wishes to reduce the response time to flyers this may be done by incorporating some form of inducement into the brochure that compels the person to act on it within a fixed period of time. For example, it may be that if the brochure is presented to the clinic within the next 2 weeks, the bearer will receive a 10% discount on the consultation. The brochure may also be used in a competition; if the reader fills out a detail slip incorporated into the brochure and returns it to the clinic, they will be eligible to win a free consultation. The details of those who are not selected as the winner can be entered into a direct mail database for further use.

Direct mail letters may also be used to target discreet client groups. Once the business has been operating for some time, and a substantial client base has been established, it's useful to divide past and present clients into demographic groups from which to construct direct mail databases. One may have a database of young families, and from this database letters may be sent to those on it containing discussions regarding seasonal or endemic children's complaints, such as exam stress or school sores, and what you can offer in response to these problems. The cost of direct mail letters is mostly related to postage and materials, and is therefore minimal.

Media Selection
The choice of the medium used to carry advertising will often be influenced by the costs involved, but one should consider a mix of media- perhaps newspaper, direct mail and radio, particularly in the first few months of the marketing campaign. The reasons for this are twofold- to maximise the chances of transmitting the marketing message to the target market, and through the

monitoring process discussed later, determine which form of advertising is the most effective in the shortest possible time.

Marketing Tools

The marketing message can be transmitted in a number of ways, and there are various means of reinforcing the message and our presence in the market place. As mentioned earlier, marketing may take the form of product or service promotion, or brand building. The tools used for marketing purposes may be used to perform either function, depending upon how they're constructed and how they're used.

Branding

For a new business, much of the marketing activity will be concerned with the promotion of the product or service that the business offers, but the importance of brand building as a key feature of all marketing processes should never be overlooked.

In this instance, the brand is essentially the name of the practice (or in some cases the practitioner) accompanied by the mystique, implications and inferences associated with the name. Branding is the marketing of that name and through this process, creating an image or mystique that becomes consistent with the name. Rolls Royce, Rolex, and Guinness are some examples of successful brand building.

Branding can greatly improve marketing efficiency. The brand usually consists of a logo, perhaps aligned with the company name, and once developed, it should be protected by a trademark. A brand should be distinctive, and should, as much as possible, communicate what is best about the business behind the brand. The brand should convey a clear and consistent point of difference to competing businesses with a high level of relevance to the audience at which it's aimed. It should denote confidence and authority, as well as quality and performance related to the product or service provided by the business.

Brand building involves reinforcing community awareness of the business and its prominence of the brand should increase as the business grows. As it grows, the brand will become associated with the quality, service, care and results for which the practice becomes known.

The importance of a brand can be illustrated by the fact that once a brand has been established, either locally or nationally, one may go broke, lose the business or be subject to almost any other calamity, but as long as the brand has not been devalued, one can use it to rebuild the entire business. To quote the president of Coca Cola, "If some unforeseen circumstance contrived to take away all our plant and offices, all our trucks and vending machines, all our licences and contracts, but left us just with our trademark (i.e., the brand), we'd get it all back within five years." (Financial Review, January 24, 1997). To further illustrate the power of the brand, the most popular tattoo in the United States was until recently, the Harley Davidson motorcycle logo. This is now losing ground to the Nike tick.

Image
Image is probably the single most powerful tool used in marketing- it permeates every facet of marketing and forms much of the subliminal signalling content provided by marketing tools. The image one projects should be seamless and continuous through everything one does. The colours one uses should be consistent throughout- signs, business cards, brochures, logo, clinic uniforms if worn by staff, the paint on the walls of the clinic- should all be constant and unwavering. Typefaces used in all written material, including signs, should be consistent. Every time someone sees this colour or print typeface, they should think of your clinic. Marketing demands that you are prominent and easily identifiable in your marketplace, and this is very difficult to achieve without a consistent image. The success of companies such as McDonald's can be blamed in large part on their consistency of image.

What that image is should be determined by what you want to say about yourself or the clinic. The central theme may be invigorating, it may be soothing, it may be clinical, but whatever the theme may be, it should also be professional. All of these messages can be conveyed with the correct image.

It should also be remembered that image extends beyond the clinic to your clothing, the type and condition of vehicle you use, the language you use- both verbal ad non-verbal, where you live, where you're seen and with whom. All of these things can all impact upon your image.

Slogan
Slogans are more commonly found among businesses that are more aggressive than healthcare practices, but their power to communicate should not be overlooked. The slogan should be short and succinct- normally a maximum of 6 words is used. The slogan can be a statement that embodies your core goal in practice and succinctly expresses your unique advantages to the community, and the slogan can be used to form the central theme of your marketing.

Clinic Name
The power of a business name should never be underestimated. The name is often the first and only thing that anyone hears in reference to a clinic, and it has the potential to stimulate attempts at contact if properly constructed.

The bulk of practice names use little more than the location of the practice, the name of the practitioner, or the healing modality practiced. They rarely take advantage of the potential that a business name has for marketing purposes, but when they do, it can contribute directly to the success of the business. Business names can highlight points of difference, competitive advantages and through the use of logos and other visual imagery, support the main marketing themes used by the business.

The name should be unique, concise, may incorporate the name of the principal practitioner or reflect the main selling point associated with the practice. Names that stand out as good choices among non-medical healthcare practices are Beaming with Health, a clinic operated by Naturopath Mim Beam in Sydney, and the Back in Motion Family Chiropractic Clinic in Brisbane.

Logo
Logo's are often thought of as being of little use to anyone other than those operating large businesses. However, like the clinic name, they can be powerful image promotion tools, and as part of a considered approach to marketing, provide strong support as brand builders. Like the clinic name the logo should be unique, encompass what you do and present this powerfully and passionately. Good logos should be protected by trademarks.

Telephone Number
Little use is made in Australia of telephone numbers as marketing tools. American businesses have been using them for quite some time with good results. A prominent American homoeopathic medicine manufacturer uses the telephone number 1800 ARNICA as its' ordering number, and the ease with which this number is remembered has added greatly to the success of this business. There's no reason why similar things cannot be done here in Australia, and for twenty seven dollars, Telstra can arrange to have a specific telephone number provided for a clinic, as long as that number has not already been allocated to another customer.

Signs
Most commercial districts allow signs to be placed in a main window or outside the premises. Signage, if properly crafted, can be very useful. Its best application is to alert passers by to your presence, many of whom will be in or on some form of motor vehicle, often moving fairly quickly past the clinic. For this latter reason they need to be eye catching and deliver a brief and succinct message. Frequently, awning signs will consist of 1 word- "Naturopath", "Osteopath" etc, to display the nature of the practice. It should be kept in mind that someone sitting in a vehicle travelling past the clinic at forty to sixty kilometres per hour will rarely have time to take in more than one word.

Where window signage is aimed at foot rather than road traffic, more text, perhaps outlining the function of the practice, hours of operation and the names of the practitioners involved, could reasonably be used. Care should be taken here to ensure that the text colour is in direct contrast with its background, otherwise it can be difficult to read. The text and background should be in keeping with whatever corporate colours are used. It may also be a good idea to have the sign painted onto a medium such as clear perspex and hung immediately behind the window. In the event that the window may be broken, this can alleviate the expense of having to replace the sign writing as well as the window glass.

As a means of attracting attention, some businesses have made use of small freestanding signs on the footpath outside the premises, painted with a white background with the top and bottom of the sign painted in blue and white hatching. These are identical in many respects to those signs used by the Police department to alert motorists that they have just passed a speed detection camera, and are very noticeable. Other businesses employ free standing signs that are centrally hinged and spin on their vertical axis in the wind, with the message painted in large letters on both sides. These are excellent at attracting attention, but are reliant on sufficient wind being present to turn them.

Business Cards
Several years ago it was fashionable in some parts of the world for business people to exchange gold business cards. Unfortunately, this period didn't last very long, but it highlighted the need to make business cards noticeable, if not valuable. The business card has a long history, but has recently, like most other marketing tools, had to work much harder to achieve its aims. Business cards often do little more than reinforce your contact details, but with some thought, can go somewhat further than this.

The understanding of normal visual physiology has been of great use in the efficient design of things such as business cards. For the standard business card shape, visual scanning follows relatively predetermined paths, and this knowledge can be used to increase the efficiency of these items. Scanning normally starts in the top left hand corner, and then tracks to information blocks which are aligned either vertically or horizontally. Because the brain prefers scanning in a consistent direction, the alignment of text should be consistent. Information of a similar nature should be grouped together- contact details, qualifications, services provided etc scan more efficiently when placed into discreet areas. When considering font size, allowance should be made for those who are vision impaired, and if the visually impaired are dealt with on a regular basis, it may be useful to incorporate Braille text into the card.

One should try to be innovative with business cards, and should not feel confined to the normal 90 by 55mm dimensions. Cards that fold out horizontally or vertically can allow for greater creativity, as can cards that carry holograms or a mixture of materials rather than just plain cardboard. Opportunities also exist to impregnate cards with essential oils and experiment with different textures of card.

Again, the image conveyed by a business card should be consistent with the rest of the image used throughout the business, and one should avoid using over-labels if changing the text or contact details on the card.

Clinic Brochures

Clinic brochures differ from direct mail brochures or flyers in that they are more permanent, they outline the overall activities and values of the clinic, and can help to introduce the clinic staff and allow the reader to more closely identify with the clinic and the practitioners. They're often left with supporting businesses to encourage referrals, and given to clients who may wish to pass them to friends or relatives. They act as envoys on your behalf- introducing you and the clinic to prospective clients, and reinforcing your image in and around the community.

Brochures are a relatively serious investment- a significant amount of cost may be involved in the design and printing of these items so they should be properly planned at the outset to maximise their effect and minimise the need to have later changes made. Clinic brochures are normally produced in the form of a 3 way fold in A4 size sheet, printed in full colour on high quality paper. The brochure should clearly outline your competitive advantages over any other local business offering similar services.

Effective brochures commonly employ the following elements:
- On the front of the brochure, a picture of the clinic accompanied by the name and contact details of the clinic, and the hours of operation, clinic logo, competitive advantages and slogan if appropriate.
- Inside the brochure:
  - A brief explanation of the main modalities offered by the clinic, accompanied by relevant full colour pictures.
  - A brief biography of the practitioner, accompanied by a (current) full colour picture.
  - Health funds offering rebates on the services provided by the clinic.
- On the back of the brochure should be a simple map, marking major roads leading to the clinic, outlining the clinics' geographical relationship to local landmarks, public transport routes, travel times from various well known landmarks, shopping centres etc, and a repetition of the clinic logo.

Given the sheer weight of advertising and marketing material most people have thrust upon them, one shouldn't necessarily expect that people are going to open a brochure. It's for this reason that the critical information- who you are, where you are, and how people can get to you, should appear on the outside of the brochure. It's also important to remember that the more written information the brochure carries, the less most people are likely to read it. Pictures and other graphic items should be heavily represented in brochures.

Yellow Pages
During the establishment period of the clinic, Yellow Pages advertising may be responsible for around fifty to eighty percent of the client intake, and it's undoubtedly one of the best investments one can make. It's normally the first place that people will look when they're seeking your services. It's operating twenty four hours per day seven day a week in every household and business across the area it covers, and it can accommodate a reasonable level of creativity.

Yellow Pages ads are not cheap (a standard 41 by 14mm column ad may cost in the area of $1000), but as the publishers own audits have shown, they are very effective.

There are a number of forms that Yellow Pages advertising can take. A single line entry in the Yellow Pages is free, but the publishers must be contacted to secure the listing. Having done this, efforts may be made by the publishers from time to time to have you upgrade your listing to a larger, paid entry. The next level of advertising above the single line may be to secure a listing in a block advertisement which is paid for by one's association. The fee for this service is usually paid to the association, and the cost is normally less than one what would normally have to pay for this level of visibility if dealing directly with Yellow Pages.

The next level of advertising, and one which often provides the best cost to benefit ratio, is a reverse block ad. These are shown in the back of the Yellow Pages and are available in various sizes, one of the most popular being the 41 by 14 mm size. One of the most effective formats in this size is the block ad with the location of the clinic in reversed block print, also known as, in column, directional format advertisements. Subject to cost constraints, one may wish to go to a larger display ad, thereby creating a higher level of visibility and accessing larger space in which to insert more graphics and text.

The text used in the ad will obviously be influenced by the space available, but the essential elements are the contact details, hours of operation, services provided, and if the space allows, a succinct expression of one's competitive advantages- your level of experience, easy access to the clinic, parking, close to shops etc. Any graphics used should be captivating and interesting and enhance activities that will promote contact. It should be kept in mind that people access the Yellow Pages because they've already recognised a need for your type of service. That part of the marketing job has already been done- now they just need to pick the person or practice that can most conveniently satisfy those requirements. Therefore, the ad should clearly show why the reader should contact you, rather than anyone else in the category. Once again, one should be aware of the needs of the reader, and ensure that the ad transmits the impression that you are the best equipped to meet these needs.

Other important considerations here are closure and publication dates of the Yellow Pages. One needs to be aware of these and time your marketing activities accordingly. For example, if you plan to begin operating a clinic in July and are relying on your Yellow pages ad for business, and the new edition of the Yellow Pages containing your ad doesn't emerge until February of the following year, you may experience some difficulty during your first six months of operation. The closure and publication dates are different for each state and region. For more information on this form of advertising, contact the publishers, Pacific Access, on 132378.

Newsletters
These work in a similar way to direct mail letters, are often used once the business has been established as a means of communicating with past and present clients, and can also be used to introduce new or prospective clients to the clinic. Fairly sophisticated newsletters can be produced with things such as dedicated publishing software, or more simply with standard word processing software.

They can be used to transmit information about:
• Topical health issues.
• Upcoming health events.
• Imminent seasonal health problems for which you should be consulted.
• Anecdotes from the clinic.
• Diets, exercises and other self-help tools.
• Brief descriptions of clinical cases that highlight your ability to assist with specific conditions.

One should ensure that the image that appears throughout the newsletter, the content and language used is consistent with the clinic image.

Vouchers
Vouchers may be offered for sale to existing clients to be used as gifts for friends or relatives for massages, iridology consultations, and naturopathic, herbal or homoeopathic consultations. They offer good opportunities to expand one's clientele, and it may be useful to advertise them just prior to Christmas.

Miscellaneous Marketing Tools
Local lectures. Use should be made of the clinic if the space is available, or local halls and other areas where you may be able to attract groups of potential clients for the purpose of lectures on your chosen modality, or of health topics that are of interest to the local community, to which you can provide solutions. Market

research should be able to indicate what these health topics may be, and one should strive to become an expert on these topics. One should be prepared to book consultations at the end of these events so that the interest that they create is not lost. If appropriate, it's also useful to hold lectures and workshops for local pharmacy and health food staff, local daycare and crèche staff, support groups for cancer, arthritis, or other common conditions, as well as groups such as nursing mothers. There are several elements to a successful lecture, and these are centred around 3 essential features

- *Engage the audience*- whilst you maintain control over the event, you should attempt to involve them in discussing salient points in the lecture- points that will serve to illustrate your knowledge of the subject, and willingness and ability to deal with it using your skills and aptitudes. Your willingness to interact should be obvious to the audience from the outset. For example, rather than open a lecture with, "Tonight I'm going to tell you why natural medicine is so important...", one may wish to begin with, "Why do you think natural medicine is so important?" This communication will be encouraged by your use of hand gestures and body language, your enthusiasm and confidence and the use of a conversational style. The use of lecterns and a professorial appearance should be avoided.
- *Tell a story rather than give a lecture*, making liberal use of your own clinical experiences, without, of course, betraying any client confidence. The audience should be told what they're about to hear, and at the end they should be reminded of what they've just heard, and the main points should be reiterated and reinforced within the context of the audiences own experiences. Whilst the lecture should take the form of a story, it should be properly structured, and its progress should be easy to follow. Like many stories, it should end with a take home message that results in the audience being inspired to make use of your services, and a means of easily accessing those services.
- *Use clear language* that is easily understood by the audience. Where possible and if appropriate, you should present the topic using as much of the local idiom as is suitable, and speak at the same pace as that commonly used by your audience. In giving these lectures, one should be outspoken but ethical and professional, stand by one's principles and not be afraid to broadcast them in a responsible manner that serves the community.

Some other points to consider are:
- Avoid reading from notes.
- Avoid descending into a monotone.
- Do not run over time.
- If taking questions from the audience, avoid being defensive if you come up against a difficult or awkward question.
- If the person asking the question cannot be heard by the audience, repeat the question.
- Do not read from overhead transparencies or projected slides.

- Use humour where it's appropriate.
- Ensure that you stick to the point and avoid drifting off into other areas, particularly as a result of answering a question that isn't directly related to the discussion topic. Such things are best answered after the lecture.

Other tools. An enormous number of items and concepts have been employed by marketers to promote or build a brand. Of these, some of the more enduring have been things such as:

- mugs
- clothing (hats and t-shirts etc)
- bumper stickers
- pens
- fridge magnets
- key rings
- calendars
- Christmas cards and birthday cards, which provide a useful means of maintaining contact.

Bulk Buy Deals

There may be scope to sell package deals where this is appropriate. For example, a bodyworker specialising is stress-release massage may consider advertising a package deal where the treatment may consist of 10 massages, but if the client buys the full package, they may, for example, receive the 10th massage session free. Some practitioners also make use of family discount packages where, rather than billing all of the members of a family individually, if the whole family book in they perhaps receive a 15% discount.

You Are Your Best Marketing Tool

Despite the breadth and diversity of marketing tools, the greatest potential for attracting new business resides within ourselves. We have the ability to promote the clinic everywhere we go. The qualities required for this activity may need to be cultivated and may be difficult to maintain, but are essential for the success and longevity of the business. The requirements here may consist of things such as:

- enthusiasm
- consistency
- professionalism
- commitment
- tolerance
- perseverance
- the ability to keep one's goals in sight

Of all of these, enthusiasm may be the most difficult thing to maintain. Fortunately, there are things that one can do to sustain this, and these are discussed in the last chapter.

As important if not more so, is the ability to deliver the desired result to clients. Efficiently assisting in the clients return to good health, coupled with an enthusiastic, caring and professional attitude, will frequently cause clients to feel obliged to suggest to their friends and family that they may also benefit from your skills. As time goes by, referrals from existing or past clients, otherwise known as "word of mouth" referrals, will become a very important source of new clients. As a point of etiquette, it's useful to send a letter of thanks to the person who referred the new client to you.

The Marketing Budget

It's useful to set aside a certain percentage of the turnover (perhaps 5%) or a certain amount of money each month to devote to marketing. If one is expecting growth or even just sustainability, marketing is very important. It may be helpful here to recall the fact that after the global depression of the 1930's, virtually the only businesses that survived were the ones who continued to advertise, and corporate research has shown that on average, every dollar spent on advertising generates three dollars in revenue.

Monitoring

Monitoring the Campaign

Once all of the activities mentioned above have been carried out and a marketing plan (discussed in more detail later) has been put into action, it's essential to monitor its success and make whatever adjustments are required to improve its effectiveness. This is particularly important in the first few months after the inception of the marketing campaign. Given the fact that the initial market research activities may be constrained by the available finances, some of the decisions made in the marketing plan may be based on guesswork rather than fact. Whilst this is obviously not desirable, monitoring the results of the marketing campaign as it progresses will provide a more objective indication as to whether the decisions made were correct.

To do this one simply needs to ask those who ring the clinic to discuss the booking of a consultation, or are making other enquiries, where they heard about the clinic. It may be useful here to the take the example of a newly established practice where word of mouth referrals have yet to make an impact. It may be that the practitioner has been running weekly ads in the local paper, talking on the local radio station, sending out direct mail flyers, encouraging referrals from the local pharmacy, running an ad in the Yellow Pages and has had outdoor advertising signs erected. Over the space of 1 month, monitoring telephone enquiries has revealed that from a total or 57 calls, the callers were motivated to contact the clinic because of the following:

	News paper	Radio	Flyers	Ph'cy	Yellow Pages	Outdoor	Total
No. of calls	10	3	4	15	21	4	57
Percentage	18	5	7	26	37	7	100

It is clear from these results that the main sources of client interest have come from 3 areas: the local newspaper, the local pharmacy and Yellow Pages advertising. If this situation were to persist for another month, it would be prudent to consider ceasing activities on the radio, and curtailing outdoor advertising. Since the nature of direct mail is such that people are generally slower to respond to it than they are to other media, unless it involves some special incentive that only applies for a short period, it may be sensible to continue this for a while longer before decisions are made regarding its future. Given the cost of advertising, one should be prepared to make fairly rapid changes to the media mix that maximises the return on the investment.

Over time, the Yellow Pages and word of mouth will become the main sources of referral, but for the first few years, other forms of advertising apart from the Yellow Pages will be essential. However, it's still important to continue monitoring the sources of referral to ensure that one remains aware of the sources of one's new clients, and it's essential to ensure that word of mouth continues to be a major area of referrals. If this declines, one needs to seriously consider the reasons why.

Monitoring the Marketplace
It's vital to monitor the success of marketing and advertising activities, but it's also essential to monitor the marketplace generally. This needs to be done constantly to stay abreast of new developments in diagnosis or therapy or other health related issues that are being discussed in the media and around the local community. This can be done by keeping up to date with events reported in the local press and other means of pubic communication, as well as staying in touch with one's colleagues and the local health food and pharmacy retailers.

One should also monitor events in the local community such as the arrival of new practitioners who may present some form of competition, and others who may have skills or tools that can be of benefit to your practice. More broadly, one should stay abreast of changes to the local economic and social climate, as well as changes to any local, state or federal laws or regulations that may affect one's practice.

The local marketplace should be monitored for any new opportunities that one may be able to take advantage of, the availability of new tools or training, and be able to capitalise on these things. It may be that a commonly used pharmaceutical product has been receiving bad publicity or has been withdrawn, and you have a safe and natural solution that may take its place.

It's also useful to consider any current or prospective developments that are likely to affect the marketplace in two, five or even ten years into the future. One's approaches to marketing and indeed one's entire business strategy, skills and aptitudes needs to be flexible enough to confidently and comfortably accommodate this future.

Marketing Plan
Having identified the major elements involved in marketing, one can then formulate a marketing plan, whereby all of these elements, or those deemed to be appropriate, can be set into a logical order and acted upon. This plan is carried out in two parts- market research and the marketing action plan.

Market Research
This involves two processes.
1. *Identify the demographic and define the target area.* As discussed above, this involves an identification of the typical client, as well as ensuring that sufficient numbers exist within the target area to ensure commercial viability.
2. *Describe the demographic.* To know how to target one's marketing activities, one must be able to describe one's main demographic or market sector- those people whose needs one is able to satisfy. One needs to know what their concerns are and how to speak to them in their own language, and at a time and place when they're most receptive to this communication. In this way, one can construct marketing activities in a way that maximises their suitability for consumption by the market sector. With the knowledge of their predominant attitudes and motivators, one will know how to formulate the marketing message, what to appeal to, and how to meet the needs of the market in a way that is immediately obvious to them. In describing the archetypal client, the factors that need to be identified are:
* The person's age range.
* The person's social and educational background.
* The person's sex.
* The person's attitudes to health.
* The person's attitude to your particular modality.
* The person's family status.
* The health needs of this sector- It's obviously important here to ensure that you have the skills and aptitudes to satisfy those requirements.
* What are their predominant health concerns and fears?
* What health problems commonly occur in the community?

- What influences them to seek the services that you're capable of providing?
  - Is it cost?
  - Is it fear of illness?
  - Is it a desire to be seen to partake in the same activities of one's peers, to subscribe to the current fashion?
- What form of marketing media is most likely to reach them?
  - Do they read the local newspapers or magazines?
  - Do they listen to the local radio station?
- Do they visit points of referral such as the local gym, health food store or pharmacy?

Sources of this information include such things as census data, medical journal articles on the levels of interest in non-medical health solutions (such as that by MacLennan et al mentioned above) as well as local health food stores, pharmacies and other local health care professionals. This analysis may reveal that in the local area surveyed, the main demographic sector consists mainly of 24 to 65 year old well educated middle class women with children, whose main health concerns are their children's health, aging and longevity, reproductive issues, and who have an active interest in natural and complementary medicine.

Marketing Action Plan
1. Identify aims.
In most cases it's useful to have a reason for one's actions; to define goals and identify a discernible path towards those goals. It may be that one aims to capture a certain portion of a market sector within a given period of time. For example, it may be that one wishes to increase client intake by 20% over a 12 month period. In any case, there should be an aim to the marketing plan, and the goals should be realistic and attainable.

2. Determine what you want to say to the demographic.
Using your knowledge of the needs of the market, match these with your competitive advantages and formulate a message that most efficiently and succinctly transmits what you want to say. It's also very useful to know who makes the decisions about health choices. For example, if one is specialising in paediatric care, is the primary decision maker the mother or the father of the child? The message should be constructed in a manner that appeals specifically to the decision maker, in a way that they can identify with. Formulate a message that will successfully communicate your ability to meet the target markets defined needs and wants. Remember that the marketplace should be able to identify with you and your message. The message should attract attention, appeal to the needs of the market, offer an attractive solution to those needs and provide a means of contact.

3. Determine the best method of communicating with the target market.
Using the information gained from the market research, determine the media that
gives you the best exposure to the target market, at the best cost per impact and
determine the required number of repetitions of the message.
4. Identify the costs involved and ensure that you have adequate funding to
support the marketing campaign. Also ensure that you are able to fund an
ongoing marketing budget.
5. Test the campaign.
An advertising company will frequently use focus groups- people taken from the
target market, to test the suitability of an advertising campaign for the target
market. As this process can be expensive, one may be able to form such a group
from friends, family or colleagues, as a means of testing the marketing campaign.
If the campaign meets with the approval of this group, it should then be put into
action.
6. Begin the advertising campaign.
7. Monitor the results and make adjustments as required.
8. Continue monitoring and adjusting as required.

Marketing Plan Example
A marketing plan for Norman Happy's Herbal Clinic (a fictitious clinic generated
for the purpose of this and other exercises in this book) may look like this:

Market Research Results
An attempt was made to define the archetypal herbal medicine client. After
consulting various scientific journal articles and talking with retailers of herbal
over the counter products (Helen's Health Foods, Ho's Healthy World Health
Foods and Phil's Pharmacy), it was found that the group most frequently using
herbal medicines were twenty five to seventy year old females. It was also
determined that these women were buying products for a broad range of health
problems, most notably PMS, digestive disorders, arthritis, skin complaints and
menopause.

They generally appear to be well educated and middle class and are mostly either
married with grown children or single, also often with grown children. They
appear to have a high level of disposable income, and their primary means of
transport are cars, although they do make use of public transport. Around two
thirds of these women were in full or part time employment. Their health
concerns centred around their appearance, about the development of chronic
disease, and the health of their children. Their retail health product buying
patterns (frequently the higher profile, more expensive brands) tend to indicate
that they buy on the basis of perceived quality and credibility rather than price.
They also appear to buy on the basis of new clinical research that is discussed in
the local print media. It was apparent that they, rather than their partners, were
the main decision makers when it came to the purchase of goods and services

related to family healthcare. They are interested in natural therapies, tend to purchase "natural" and many have also expressed a desire to consult a professional herbalist.

Having examined the local print media, viewed their readership figures and contacted the businesses running advertising in these media to check these figures, it was determined that that target market was most likely to read the local newspaper, The Happy Hill Herald, and national magazines, Women's Weekly and New Idea. They also tended to listen to the local AM radio station, 4AA, and were particularly vigilant during Healthy Kev's health and wellbeing program, aired on Monday nights from 7.30 to 8.30 p.m. Discussions with Happy Hill Direct mail indicated that this sector also responded well to direct mail. Further discussions with some of their clients confirmed this view.

After talking with a large number of local retailers of non- health product and service providers, it became clear that due to the size and density of the commercial district, and the paucity of public parking facilities, car parking and access to public transport were major local issues. It was also apparent that the extremes of temperature experienced in the Happy Hill area made access to air conditioned premises a high priority. The main method by which the target market makes enquiries regarding products or services is by telephone. The Internet is a little-used communication method.

Market Area
Having driven by car for a period of twenty minutes in every direction from the clinic, a circular area was defined. Local council area census figures determined that this area was inhabited by approximately 48,000 people, living permanently in approximately 16,000 dwellings. Of these 48,000 people, approximately 12,000 fit within the described target market.

Marketing Action Plan
Aims
The aim is to generate a client intake of 10%, or 1,200 people from the target area within the first 2 years of operation.

The Marketing Message
The elements of the marketing message will include the following:
• A means of attracting the attention of the target market to marketing.
• A focus on the clinics competitive advantages.
• Easy parking and air conditioned premises.
• University trained and experienced herbalist.
• An offer of solutions to health concerns.
• Evidence based natural solutions to women's health problems and conditions related to aging.

- A means of telephone contact.

The means by which the message will be transmitted will be the Happy Hill Herald, one ad per week for a trial period of seven weeks, situated in the top right hand corner of page three. Two 15 second ads per week for a trial period of seven weeks will also be aired on Healthy Kev's radio program, one played at 7.35, and the other immediately prior to the 8.00pm news break. The radio station, through Healthy Kev's producer, has approved two interviews with Norman Happy to be conducted by Healthy Kev during this seven week period, at no cost. Direct mail will be delivered to a defined area comprising of 10% of the target area, once per week delivered on a Monday morning, for a trial period of seven weeks.

Print advertisements and direct mail flyers will be written by Norman Happy and radio ads will be written by Norman Happy and recorded by Healthy Kev.

The two health food stores and one pharmacy mentioned above have been approached and have approved two half day in-store customer advice sessions, with the proviso that a certain amount of stock is sold during these sessions. They have also given approval for further sessions, once a week for the next seven weeks, on the basis that sales reach the agreed level for each session.

A 40 by 14mm reverse block ad will be published in the Yellow Pages telephone directory, the release of which will coincide with the beginning of the marketing campaign.

Costs
The costs of the 7 week campaign are as follows:
Happy Hill Herald advertising- $300.00
4AA radio advertising- $700.00
Direct Mail flyers- printing and distribution $792.00
Yellow Pages advertising $1000.00
          Total cost $2792.00
Funding is available to meet this amount.

Testing the Campaign
Prior to formalising the arrangements mentioned above, the print ads, direct mail flyers and radio ads will be discussed with a focus group formed from students of the Norma Happy School of Creative Dance. The focus group will be made up of ten women whose backgrounds are similar to that of the target market and the campaign will proceed only after it receives the approval of the majority of this focus group. Any comments, agreed to by the majority of the group, suggesting improvements on any part of this campaign will be acted upon prior to the

launch of the campaign. The cost of appropriating the services of the focus group will be negligible as each participant will be offered twenty percent off the price of an introductory progressive Rumba class. The campaign will then be put into place and the results constantly monitored over the next seven weeks, at the end of which, the necessary adjustments will be made.

It should be noted from this example that it may be difficult to sustain these costs (nearly $400 per week) for an extended period of time. Realistically, after the results from each form of advertising have been assessed at the end of the 7 week period, one may well simply maintain the Yellow Pages advertising and the other single most effective means of advertising.

12. Financial and Business Management
Financial Management
Failure to properly monitor and manage the finances is one of the most common reasons for businesses to collapse. One can be the best practitioner and marketer in the country, but unless things such as cash flow, debt level, stock level and profitability are managed efficiently and punctually, those skills will mean very little. The key to financial management is monitoring- being aware of the current financial position of the business and being able to see what's likely to happen in the future. In this way, problems can be managed before they become unmanageable, and opportunities can be taken advantage of. The tools that may be used here include such things as cash flow analyses, forecasting, profit and loss calculations and balance sheets, which will be discussed in this chapter.

This section of the text is not designed to turn the reader into an accountant, merely to simplify some of the more important factors that relate the financial management of a non-medical healthcare practice. For more detailed financial advice, the services of a qualified accountant or financial advisor should be sought.

Transaction Record
This is a rendering of the raw trading data involved in the operation of the business, detailing the ebb and flow of funds going into and out of the business. The details recorded go to produce a broad number of reports, statements and ratio analyses, and they are essential for the purposes of daily, weekly, quarterly and annual reconciliation and reports. For the purposes of daily cash reconciliation, it may be useful if actual cash transactions are marked in some way, to differentiate them from other forms of exchange such as credit cards and cheques.

The two main features of cash flow recordings are income or credits (money received for goods or services provided) and expenses or debits (money leaving the business to pay for the expenses incurred by the business). These amounts are entered into a software program such as Quicken or MYOB, or into a manually entered "cash book" as they occur, and a running record kept of the current financial state of the business.

In a tabular form, the weekly figures may look something like the following.

The Happy Herbalist- Cash Book Accounts- August 2003

Date	Credits			Debits								Bal.
	Goods	Consults	Total	Stock	Utilities	Wage	Marketing	Loan	Rent	Tax	Total	
Aug 1	200	400	600				50		250		300	300
Aug 2	275	510	785									785
Aug 3	100	220	320									320
Aug 4	180	270	450									450
Aug 5	205	355	560	525		590					1115	(555)
Aug 8	250	500	700				50		250		300	400
Aug 9	50	100	150									150
Aug 10	375	750	1125									1125
Aug 11	75	150	225									225
Aug 12	200	400	600			590		100			690	(90)
Aug 15	275	550	825				50		250		300	525
Aug 16	125	250	375		450						450	(75)
Aug 17	200	400	600									600
Aug 18	225	450	675									675
Aug 19	175	350	525	1650		590				3750	5990	(5465)
Aug 22	350	700	1050				50		250		300	750
Aug 23	250	500	750									750
Aug 24	250	500	750									750
Aug 25	300	600	900									900
Aug 26	250	500	750		300	590		100			990	(240)
Aug 29	200	400	600				50		250		300	300
Aug 30	325	650	975									975
Aug 31	125	250	375									375
Total	4960	9755	14715	2175	750	2360	250	200	1250	3750	6985	3980

The figures in brackets represent a loss, and note that no allowance has been made here for dividends or payments made to shareholders.

In this example, at the end of the month of August the cash position or gross profit is at $3930.00. It should be kept in mind here that these figures only represent 1 months trading. They do not include insurance, bad debts, depreciation, payments to shareholders or sundry expenses. The apparent poor return is due principally to the taxation payment made in this month, which will average out over the course of the year.

As the months and years go by and one continues to record this data, it should be analysed for things such as seasonal fluctuations, and steps should be taken in the areas such as marketing to reduce these fluctuations. It should also be closely monitored for the following:

Rising expense levels. It can be useful to plot these separately and look at each month as a percentage change on the previous month, and when more historical data becomes available, look at each month as a percentage of the same month during the previous year, and the year before that, and so on. Naturally, as the volume of business increases, so will the levels of expenditure. However, as your systems improve and efficiency levels increase, the expense level per client should decrease. For example, if one were to pick the figures from the week beginning August 1 from the cash book entries above, and plot them against the numbers of clients seen per week (given that the medicines supplied to each person were all of the same value), an analysis of the expense levels per client for each week may look like this):

The Happy Herbalist- Client Expense Analysis

Week Beginning	No. Clients Seen	Expenses	Expense per Client	% Change on Previous Year
1 Aug 2001	15	726	$48.40	0
1 Aug 2002	24	1008	$42.00	86.8
1 Aug 2003	35	1415	$40.40	96.2

The expense per client is calculated by dividing the weeks expenses by the number of clients seen in that week. This analysis essentially reflects the cost of seeing a client. Given that all expenses are represented, the results are fairly clear. This analysis may be done on a monthly instead of a yearly basis if necessary, or can be done to compare one year with the previous year and so on. It can also be performed on individual expense categories if required, and if a problems exists, it can be more easily identified and dealt with. An improvement in profitability will be shown by a percentage of less than 100% as compared with the previous period. If this figure should rise above 100%, it indicates an increase in the cost of seeing a client, and this should be dealt with.

Falling levels of profitability. Profitability is the ability of the practice to make a profit, after expenses have been subtracted. If this falls, it will be either because of a rise in expenses that are not the result of an increase in income, or because of a fall in income. The cause needs to be discovered and dealt with.

Static levels of profitability. This should be monitored, and if it continues for 3 or more months, should be addressed as if it were a fall in profitability. Given the constantly rising costs of being in business, if one's own profitability is not growing, it's failing to keep up with the commercial environment around it and, in reality, going backwards. For example, if the rate of inflation and the CPI were around 3%, any business with a profitability increase of less than 3% is essentially going backwards.

Profitability
The level of profit when viewed in isolation says little about the performance of a business. In order to evaluate profit levels in realistic terms, it needs to be compared and related to other aspects of the business. To put it into perspective, profit should be compared with factors such as:
• The amount of total assets tied up in the business.
• The shareholders capital invested in the business.
• Sales revenue.

Return on assets. This is the net profit earned expressed as a percentage of the total assets used. For example, if, in the above example, the value of the assets amounted to $25,143, and profit made by the business for the year amounted to $42,000, this represents a return on assets of 167%. (42,000 divided by 25143 x 100)

Return on investment. This is the amount of net profit earned expressed as a percentage of the owners equity in the business. Again, using the example above, with the owners equity being at $12,567, and a profit figure of $42,000, the return on investment would be 334%. (42,000 divided by 12,567, multiplied by 100)

Forecasting
Forecasts are essential financial management tools, and include such things as expense forecasts and cash flow forecasts. The accuracy of the forecast will be affected by extraordinary expenses and seasonal fluctuations, although this latter consideration should become clearer as the business progresses and more data becomes available. The value of forecasts is somewhat limited due to the fact that they involve a certain amount of guesswork, but are as close to the probable financial future as is able to be had. The more effort that is put into development of a forecast the greater its usefulness and value is likely to be.

Expense forecasts. These are useful as a means of ensuring that one has adequate funds to meet future requirements. When these future expenses are clearly laid out, allowances can be made for them and budgets can be constructed to allow for their payment. An expense forecast schedule may look something like the following.

The Happy Herbalist- Expense Forecast Schedule Tax Year 2003-2004

Month	Wage	Marketing	Utilities	Sundries	Stock	Insurance	Loan	Tax	Rent	Total
July	2557	1200	750	200	2000	560	200		1083	8550
Aug	2557	200		200	2000		200	3750	1083	9990
Sept	2557	200		200	2000		200		1083	6240
Oct	2557	200	750	200	2000		200		1083	6990
Nov	2557	200		200	2000		200	3750	1083	9990
Dec	2557	200		200	2000		200		1083	6240
Jan	2557	200	750	200	2000	560	200		1083	7550
Feb	2557	200		200	2000		200	3750	1083	9990
March	2557	200		200	2000		200		1083	6240
April	2557	200	750	200	2000		200		1083	6990
May	2557	200		200	2000		200	3750	1083	9990
Jun	2557	200		200	2000		200		1083	6240
Total	30684	3400	3000	2400	24000	1120	2400	15000	12996	95000

Note also that no allowance has been made here for acquisition of new fixed assets, the practitioners salary, dividends or payments made to shareholders.

Cash flow forecasts. These are useful predictors of when money may need to be borrowed to cover expenses, how much cash is required to keep the business running, and when money may be available for investment in marketing and other purposes. Cash flow essentially involves funds coming into and going out of the business. It should be kept in mind that cash flow statements don't show the profitability of a business, but show either a historic view from existing data, or a prediction of the flows of cash into and out of the business. Cash flow is one of the most critical things to monitor- without cash we cannot pay staff or creditors or buy stock, and if we're unable to do these things, the business will not survive. Cash flow forecasts make these types of problems apparent while there's still something that can be done about them. Various practices and procedures have been designed to increase the visibility of these factors. For the purposes of forecasting, actual data and estimates may be made using a summary version of the details derived from the cash book or equivalent software mentioned above.

An example of a cash flow forecast may look something like the following.

The Happy Herbalist- Cash Flow and Projections 2003-2004

Credits				Debits			
	Goods	Consult	Total	Total* Expenses	Net Cash Flow	Opening Balance	Closing Balance
July	5350	10700	16050	8550	7500	4350	11850
Aug	4960	9755	14715	9990	4725	11850	16575
Sept	4750	9500	14250	6240	8010	16575	24585
Oct	4275	8550	12825	6990	5835	24585	30438
Nov	6750	13500	20250	9990	10260	30438	40698
Dec	1475	2950	4425	6240	(1815)	40698	38883
Jan	2375	4750	7125	7509	(384)	38883	38499
Feb	4500	9000	13500	9990	3510	38499	42009
Mar	5500	11000	16500	6240	10260	42009	52269
Apr	5750	11500	17250	6990	10260	52269	62529
May	4625	9250	13875	9990	3885	62529	66414
Jun	6500	13000	19500	6240	13260	66414	79674

*Expenses would normally be itemised here as seen in the Expense Forecast Schedule above. Note also that no allowance has been made here for capital purchases (fixed assets) dividends or payments made to shareholders.

The figures from July to December are actual. The figures from January to June are based on estimates from data gleaned from industry averages, and the influences of seasonal fluctuations (e.g. Christmas) and the influence of the clinics promotional and marketing activities for these months.

To make the terms used somewhat clearer,

Net cash flow is calculated by taking total debits away from total credits. For example, for August, the total debit figure of $9,990 is subtracted from the total credit figure of $14,715 to give a net cash flow of $4,725.

The *opening balance* figure is arrived at by adding the cash flow and opening balance figure from previous month. For example, taking the month of August once again, the opening balance of $11,850 is derived by adding the July net cash flow of $7,500 to the July opening balance of $4,350.

The *closing balance* for the period is determined by adding the net cash flow figure to the opening balance, such as can be seen in the closing balance of $16,575 for August, where the nest cash flow of $4725 is added to the opening balance of $11,850.

Note that depreciation, which is a paper accounting transaction not involving any actual cash transaction, is not shown.

Profit and Loss Report

The profit and loss report examines a businesses trading activity for a certain time period, one month, three months, six months or a year. It displays the relationship between income and expenses, and from these, shows either profit or loss for the period examined.

The profit and loss report assists in highlighting the variables involved in profitability, and is useful in showing the net profit as a percentage of gross income. The profit and loss account differs significantly from the balance sheet discussed below in that it is a record of the clinics trading activities over a period of time, whereas the balance sheet is the financial position at one moment in time. It should also be noted that on the profit and loss table, provision is made for expenses incurred but not yet paid- these are known as accruals.

The basic calculation for determining net profit is: Net sales – (cost of goods sold + total expenses) = net profit. The percentage net profit is the net profit expressed as a percentage of net sales.

In tabular form, the profit and loss report may look something like the following:

The Happy Herbalist P&L Report for April 2002

Items	$	%
Gross income (Consultations and medicine sales)	10,860	100
Opening Stock — 6,100		
Purchases — 3500		
Closing stock — 2600		
Cost of goods sold	3500	32
Gross Profit	7380	68
Expenses		
Fixed Expenses		
Salaries — 2557		
Rent — 1083		
Power and phone — 750		
Advertising — 200		
Loan — 180		
Other — 55		
Variable expenses		
Accruals (tax) — 1250		
Stationery — 15		
Other — 10		
Total Expenses	6100	56
Net Profit	$1280	12%

Note also that no allowance has been made here for depreciation (normally included under Fixed Expenses), retained profit, dividends or payments made to shareholders.

Balance Sheet
The balance sheet is a financial statement outlining the financial position of the business, and for small businesses it's normally constructed at the end of the financial year to outline the financial position of the business at that time. Essentially, it sets out what the business owes and what it owns. It also gives shareholders and potential investors information about the value of the business.

There are a number of elements contained within the balance sheet.

Current assets are those things which are easily convertible into cash, or will be used within the space of one year. Current assets include cash, money owed to the business, and trading stock (e.g. dispensary stock).
Fixed assets are those things that the business will consume over a period longer than a year. It includes things such as furniture, fittings, curtains, lighting, computers, fax machines etc, the building, investments in other businesses and goodwill.

Current liabilities are debts which must be paid within one year.
Non Current liabilities are debts owed by the business that do not have to be paid within the year.
Owners equity is the balance of what the owners possess, and since this is owed by the business to the owners, it constitutes a liability.

An example of a balance sheet may look like this:

The Happy Herbalist- Balance Sheet for the year ending June 30, 2003

ASSETS		LIABILITIES	
Current Assets		Current Liabilities	
Cash on hand	650	Accounts payable	5217
Cash in bank	9254	Accrued taxation	3750
Accounts receivable	25	Total Current Liabilities	8967
Stock inventory	6205		
Total Current Assets	16134		
Fixed Assets		Non Current liabilities	
Fixtures (-depreciation)	5000	Loan repayments 2004	1800
Other fixed assets	4000	Loan repayments 2005	1800
Total Fixed Assets	9000	Total Long Term Liabilities	3600
		Total Liabilities	12567
		Net Worth	
		Owners Equity	12567
Total assets	25134	Total liabilities and net worth	25134

Financial Monitoring Ratios
There are a number of monitoring tools that look at various aspects of the account details in a ratio form, essentially providing a quick view of certain aspects of the financial health of the business.
Liquidity ratios, such as the Current ratio, reflect the ability of the business to meet short term debt requirements and access capital for investment. The Current ratio is calculated by dividing the current assets by the current liabilities. This shows the ability of a business to pay its debts if called upon to do so at short notice. Using the figures from the balance sheet above, the total current assets are $16,134, and the current liabilities are $8,967. This would produce a ratio of 1.8 (16,143 divided by 8,967). This figure should be above 1, but if it is it may indicate that money which could be used to generate income is sitting idle. Some financial analyses may also use the Acid test ratio, calculated by subtracting the stock from current assets, and then dividing this by the current liabilities. In some ways this reflects a truer picture of liquidity, particularly where stock is not immediately convertible to cash, or certainly not to the same level as which it was purchased. Ideally, the acid test ratio should be around 1.

Business activity ratios illustrate how effectively the resources are being used by the business. These consist of the Stock turnover ratio, calculated by dividing the cost of goods sold by the stock, and the Debt collection period ratio, calculated by dividing the businesses debtors by the turnover and multiplying this by 365. This ratio is expressed in days, and shows the average debt recovery period.

Profitability ratios display the level of profitability in relation to other aspects of the business, such as the amount of capital invested in the business and income. The main profitability ratios are Return on Total Assets, calculated by dividing the net profit before interest and taxes by total assets, and multiplying this result by 100. The net profit margin is determined by dividing net profit before interest and taxes by income and multiplying this result by 100. Net asset turnover is calculated by dividing income by total assets.

Monitoring Priorities
As can be seen from the discussions above, the key to financial management is vigilance. Some aspects of this may be more important than others, particularly in the short term. If one were to select the highest monitoring priorities, these should be:
*   Gross income
*   Profitability
*   Imminent expenses
*   Liquidity of the business
*   Expenditure per client
*   Stock levels
*   Stock expenditure
*   Bad debt level

Miscellaneous Issues
A discussion on financial management would not be complete without budgets. The primary considerations here are the profit and expense budgets. Budgets in this context refer to the increase in the quantity or value of something over a period of time, in this case, profit and turnover, expressed as a percentage growth or decline relative to the previous period and the budget target. The measurement of the actual results against the budget will indicate quite clearly whether the targets have been achieved. The targets set should be realistic and attainable, and for this reason, one could reasonably set higher targets for some periods than others, lower when periods of low activity may be anticipated and higher when appropriate. All of the information that relates to budgets can be used in forming annual cashflow forecasts.

An example of a budget may look something like the following.

The Happy Herbalist- Profit Budget Schedule- 2003/2004

Month	Gross income	Gross expenses	Gross profit	Budget target	% of Budget*
July	16050	8550	7500	7000	107
Aug	14715	9990	4725	5000	95
Sept	14250	6240	8010	8000	101
Oct	12825	6990	5835	6000	97
Nov	20250	9990	10260	10000	103
Dec	4425	6240	(1815)	3000	-
Jan	7125	7509	(384)	2000	-
Feb	13500	9990	3510	3000	117
March	16500	6240	10260	11000	93
April	17250	6990	10260	10000	103
May	13875	9990	3885	5000	78
Jun	19500	6240	13260	11000	121
Total	170265	94959	75306	81000	93

*this is the gross profit expressed as a percentage of the budget target

As can be seen from this schedule, unforeseen losses in the months of December and January and a poor result in May produced an overall drop in the results, causing in most part the 7% shortfall of the budget target. Generally, the results for most months were fairly close to the target. The targets for the 2004/2005 year will need to be modified to take the above results for December, January and May into consideration, or marketing strategies put into place to reduce the possibility of similar results occurring after examining the cause for these results.

Of less importance but still significant is the *expense budget*. This details the likely expenses for the coming year and is useful as a means of determining if projected income will meet the projected expenses. For the purposes of illustration, the expense forecast schedule shown above may serve as an example.

In regard to *banking*, this should be done by either the practitioner or the receptionist, at least twice weekly if not daily, to minimise the potential of loss due to burglary or robbery. Most insurance companies and police departments advise those who regularly perform this function, to:
- Vary the times at which the banking is done.
- Avoid using the same route every time to get from the clinic to the bank.
- Try to avoid using public transport.
- Keep the doors locked and avoid quiet streets if using a car to transport cash.
- Avoid quiet streets if walking to transport cash.
- Avoid carrying cash in things such as bank bags.

- Avoid discussing cash movements with those outside the clinic.

Due to the value of the clinics financial data, it's advisable to keep copies of this material off the premises in case of a fire or burglary.

Business Management
For the purposes of this discussion, business management revolves around the central issue of the business plan. The business plan may be seen as the master plan to which the marketing plan discussed earlier is subservient. Hopefully, one also has a personal plan which provides the impetus for the business plan. This personal plan may involve such things as national dominance in a particular area of chiropractic medicine. It may be to see a particular health problem permanently eradicated from the community. It may also be that one wishes to retire with five million dollars profit at the age of forty five. In any case, the function of the business should be to serve the needs of the shareholder or shareholders and so the business plan should be structured in a manner that will allow the business to fulfil those requirements.

The business plan is a document that assists in future planning, helps one to realistically examine the goals of the business, provides for the possibility of anticipating future problems and enables ideas to be tested on paper before they involve any significant expenditure. The business plan is also invaluable for the purposes of convincing potential investors or financial institutions that one's plans can be realised. In addition, it allows one a clearer perspective of competitive advantages, and the capacity to allow one to determine if one has the personal capabilities to achieve the aims of the plan.

The elements of the plan consist of the aim of the plan, the objectives of the business, discussions on the activities and structure of the business, the business environment and competition. As well as these areas, it covers the fundamentals of marketing, the background of the business operators, financial activity and future prospects as well as relevant documentation and advisors.

The Business Plan
The rudiments of the business plan are as follows:
1. Summary
- The purpose of the business plan- e.g. to acquire funding for expansion.
- Current funding requirements- if the purpose of the plan is to acquire funding.
- A description of the business- sole trader, partnership etc.
- Business profile- the nature of the business- naturopathy, acupuncture etc.
- Objectives of the business- what the business is aiming to achieve.
- Current analysis- the current financial state of the business.
- Key factors- in brief- the factors influencing the future of the business.

2. Industry Analysis
- Overview of the industry that you're in- outlining the dynamics, future prospects, threats and opportunities etc related to the industry as a whole.
- Economic trends- whether the industry is growing or contracting and why.
- Consumer trends- attitudinal and other factors influencing the industry, and the level of demand for your type of service.
- Social and/or political trends- social and political influences on your industry and the impact of government (at all levels) upon it.
- Price sensitivity of market- the importance of price in your industry and ramifications of altering prices.

3. The Business
- Resume of owner/proprietor.
- Organisation structure (sole trader, company, etc).
- Main activities of the business.
- Location of the business.
- Current level of capital.
- Unique features and competitive advantages of the business.
- Business advisors- accountant, solicitor, banker etc.
- Strengths and weaknesses of the business.
- Stock suppliers details.
- Past performance of the business.
- Current performance of business.
- Description of the products and services provided by the business.
- Current capacity- how many clients can currently be seen.
- Expansion capacity- how many clients could be seen if the premises were expanded.
- Quality control monitoring- how is the quality of the clinics output measured.
- Future requirements- equipment, material, human resources etc.

4. Competition- description of the competition
- Its strengths and weaknesses and how your business compares.
- The potential for the competition to be a threat and why.
- Discussion on the competitions market share.

5. Marketing
- Research and analysis methods.
- Target market- a description of the typical client.
- Market share- how much of the market you currently service.
- Market potential- the potential size of the market that you can access.
- Key factors influencing the market- the kinds of things that can affect the market.
- Advertising and promotion- describe the methods that are best suited to your needs.
- Marketing plan- outline the components previously described in the marketing plan.

- Monitoring- describe the means by which the marketing activities will be monitored.

6. Financial Information
- Breakeven point- describe your breakeven point in terms of the level of income required to break even and the number of clients required to generate that amount. If the purpose of the business plan is to seek funding, comment should be made on the businesses ability to break even, repay those funds and still generate an income to meet the shareholders or owners personal needs.
- Costing and pricing- outline the pricing structure of consultations, treatments of medicines, and the reasons why these prices have been selected.
- Current position- construct a profit and loss statement for the previous trading period.
- Balance sheet- construct a balance sheet outlining the current position.
- Income and expenditure projection- outline projected income and expenditure for the next trading period.
- Profit budget- outline the profit budget for the next trading period.
- Insurance- outline all current insurance policies.
- Sources of finance- detail the various options available to you for funding.
- Capital requirements- how much do you need to fulfil the goals of this business plan.
- Capital allocation- what do you plan to do with the funds.
- Timing and staging of finance- describe whether or not your plans for expansion involve a series of stages, and if so, whether the funding required is to be supplied in portions to finance each stage.

7. Management and Staffing
- Management- a description of the key management personnel.
- Duties and responsibilities- a description of the duties and responsibilities of current clinic staff.
- Staffing requirements- a description of your requirements for staff, and the reasons why they're needed

8. Supporting Documents
Copies should be supplied of:
- Legal documents.
- Leases or contracts.
- Letters of intent:
  - From suppliers, that they're happy to supply you with goods.
  - From points of referral, that they're willing to refer clients to you.
- Patents or trademarks.

9. SWOT (Strengths, Weaknesses, Opportunities and Threats) Analysis
- Outline the strengths of the business- its competitive advantages what it does that is unique in the market place.
- Outline the weakness of the business- what it needs or needs to do more of to succeed.

- Outline the opportunities, current and future, available to the business and how you plan to capitalise on these.
- Outline the threats to the business- the kinds of things that could quickly put you out of business and how you plan to protect yourself against them.

10. Action Plan
- Describe the strategies and methods by which you plan to achieve the goals of the business plan. These should be derived from the SWOT analysis, looking mainly at the areas where opportunities exist and the means by which these opportunities will be realised. The marketing plan should act as the principal tool used in this area. One should also ensure here that strategies are in place to address the strengths, weaknesses and threats. In simple terms, one may be able to:
  - Utilise strengths to capitalise on opportunities.
  - Repair weaknesses with opportunities.
  - Utilise strengths to attack weaknesses.
  - Repair weaknesses to counter threats.
- Each stage of the action plan should be monitored and a description of this monitoring process should be included.

Once the requirements outlined in the business plan have been acquired, the plan can proceed.

Exit and Succession Planning
When starting out in business one rarely gives much thought to getting out of the business, or to the notion that at some point, one may like to escape from the pressures of a life as a professional healer. Vast numbers of practitioners who have given almost their entire lives to the service of their communities have literally "died with their boots on", still working up into their 80's and beyond, not knowing how to retire while still ensuring that the needs of the community are met. It's useful therefore, to give some thought to the strategies involved in removing oneself gracefully from the practice. There are essentially two means of doing this.

The first of these involves a succession plan. After many years in practice, dealing with the same clients, their children, and perhaps their children's children, one's client community will have become used to the ways and methods of the practice, and in effect, these ways and methods become part of the practice itself. Therefore, one of the least disruptive methods of removing oneself from the practice is to train another similarly qualified practitioner in these methods, and gradually introduce this person to the client community. In this way, one can be assured that the needs of the clients continue to be met, in the manner that they have become used to. Another aspect to this is that many non-medical healthcare providers develop techniques over the years that are unique to that practitioner.

These techniques can have a great deal to offer the profession and the community, and unless these skills are handed on, their benefits may be lost for all time. The person one selects for this succession should hopefully have a similar temperament, attitude and outlook to the retiring practitioner, and be committed to carrying on a practice in the tradition originally established in the clinic. These individuals may be hard to find, and an option frequently used to facilitate this is to act as a mentor, assisting new graduates from training institutions with the establishment of their own practices. In this way, one may be able to observe at close range the persons skills and aptitudes, and their suitability for taking over the practice.

The second method of escape is to simply sell the practice. However, in doing so, one should ensure that the practitioner who purchases the clinic will be suited to the task, and all of the factors discussed in Chapter 9 (Practice Options) are taken into consideration.

Finally on this issue, those working in Victoria need to be aware of certain provisions made under the Health Records Act 2001 (Victoria). These provisions stipulate that a healthcare provider selling, transferring ownership of, or closing a practice must publish an advertisement in a newspaper or newspapers that cover the trading area, outlining the future of the clinic and what is to become of the client records held by the clinic. This advertisement must be published at least two months prior to the change in ownership or status of the practice and if clients do not use English as their main language, the advertisement will need to be published in their preferred language. This Act also has implications for situations that relate to the death of the practitioner, if they're still operating the practice immediately prior to their death. For more on this see www.health.vic.gov.au/hsc

Enterprise Review

Some time ago, a business management tool was developed for use by established organisations as a means of gauging their effectiveness in the eyes of others with whom they're involved commercially. This tool is called the enterprise review. Its function is to assess the effectiveness and direction of an organisation, from the viewpoint of those who do not own the business. One can then use this assessment as a means of improving the businesses practices and realign the organisations direction to one that is better suited to success. One may also consider this as something of a reality check. One of the things that some organisations fail to appreciate is that their view of the world is mostly from the inside of the organisation out, whereas the view should really be from the clients perspective- from the outside in. In the non-medical healthcare industry, commercial growth is much more reliant upon the clients view of the practice than it is on the practices view of the client. Failure to recognise this can lead to commercial mediocrity, if not slow decline and demise.

Enterprise reviews are not normally conducted until the business has been trading for some time, normally a minimum of 2 years, so that it has had some time to make an impression on those dealing with it. After this, enterprise reviews are often conducted every 2 to 5 years as a means of fine tuning the activities and direction of the business.

The procedure one follows here is to ask one's staff, clients, suppliers and all others with whom one has a commercial relationship, one simple question- "What can the (name of the practice, for example The Happy Herbalist) do to improve its effectiveness?" The question may vary somewhat from this or be couched in different terms, but what it seeks to capture are perceptions from as many different angles as possible, of the effectiveness of the practice and what can be done to improve it. One should assure the respondents to this question that the answers they give will be kept in strict confidence and taken as constructive criticism. In fact, for the purposes of receiving objective and honest comment, it may be useful for the principals of the business to remove themselves from this operation entirely and retain the services of a management company to carry out the process.

The comments are then collected and grouped into themes. These may be such things as problems with the telephone system, problems associated with the receptionist, or problems associated with the attitude of the practitioner. The number of comments per theme will give a good indication of the importance of that theme to the respondents. Having sorted these comments into themes, the next task is to develop action plans that will improve the function of these areas. The numbers of comments per theme will also dictate the order in which they're dealt with- obviously, the themes with the largest number of comments should receive the highest priority.

To follow the examples above, the actions developed to deal with problems with the telephone system may be to purchase or lease a new telephone system. Problems associated with the receptionist may be dealt with by objectively assessing the effectiveness of the receptionist, and with their input, if required, produce a plan for improvement. An attitudinal problem with the practitioner may be addressed by developing some form of attitudinal improvement plan for the practitioner.

The results and insights that can be gleaned from this process may be shocking, and may provoke all manner of feelings in the recipients of the comments, but the power and usefulness of such an audit should never be underestimated. Organisation that have carried out enterprise reviews have often had to take major deviations from the directions in which they have been headed, but have derived great benefit from doing so.

13. Getting Started and Staying in Business

Getting Started

Once the clinic is set up and ready to begin operating, it will be useful to have some means of generating a large amount of business in the shortest possible time, until word of mouth and resources such as Yellow Pages advertising begin to produce results. Unfortunately, the rent, insurance, power, telephone and other expenses are unlikely to wait until the appointment book is full.

Much of the information required to assist in this process can be found in the section on marketing, although other areas that are likely to generate good results in the shortest period of time are:

- Newspaper editorials- most local newspapers are usually quite willing to publish articles on business that have recently been established in the local area. The best approach here is to contact the newspaper editor and let them know your situation, clearly outlining the benefits of your practice to the community. The editor may then dispatch one of their journalists to the clinic who will conduct the interview, and may take some photographs. Once the article has been published, it can be useful to contact both the editor and the journalist and thank them for the favour. It can also be useful to encourage a relationship with the editor or the journalist, so that when a local health issue arises on which you may be able to comment, there's a good chance that you will be contacted. As with all marketing situations, it's important that you control the agenda as much as possible. It can be helpful to supply the journalist with a list of questions that will highlight the points you wish to make.

In regard to the content of the article,
- The subject or subjects discussed should only be those that are of current interest to the local community.
- Use examples of clinical success from your own practice, or from the teaching clinic where you did your clinical training.
- Don't use jargon.
- Make use of personal anecdotes with which the reader can identify.
- Keep your responses to questions succinct- most editorials are subject to space restrictions, and editorials such as these being discussed will rarely be allowed to run for more then 300 words. Ideally, one would have written the answers to the list of questions supplied, to ensure that the answer will fit within the confines of the space requirements.
- Consider suggesting a headline to the story that will attract the attention of the readers.

In regard to the photo,
- Use the most photogenic part of the clinic as a backdrop, or if this isn't suitable, using the front of the clinic may be useful.

- Avoid using props such as stethoscopes unless you have the appropriate qualifications.
- Avoid being photographed behind a desk or any other barrier.
- Dress in a manner that is consistent with your image.
- Try to look natural, friendly and professional.
- Direct mail brochures or flyers, as previously mentioned.
- Local lectures, as previously mentioned.
- Lectures or workshops for those most likely to refer clients- local pharmacy and health food staff, local daycare and crèche staff, staff from gymnasiums and other sports related centres, as well as self help groups.

Maintaining Enthusiasm

The erosion of the enthusiasm that one feels when first beginning the practice, particularly in the first twelve months if one has begun from scratch, is very common and can make life in the clinic very tedious. Unfortunately, as time passes, it can become increasingly difficult not to infect staff and clients with this feeling of tedium. There are a numbers of means by which this might be forestalled. Some of the things to keep in mind are:

- Never lose sight of your goals.
- Take regular holidays.
- Keep regular hours. The normal working week for many non-medical healthcare practitioners is Monday, Tuesday, Thursday and Friday from 8.30 am to 7 p.m., and Saturday from 8.30 am to 1 p.m. with Wednesdays normally devoted to marketing, admin, research and monitoring activities. Working after hours may be necessary from time to time, but not having clearly defined times during which one works can result in working for many more hours than is healthy, either mentally or physically.
- For the same reasons, it may become necessary to limit the number of clients one sees per day.
- Maintain regular contact with your colleagues and peers through things such as regular breakfast meetings, attendance at association functions and professional seminars.
- Develop and maintain peer networks.
- Speak on your chosen modality at professional seminars.
- Subscribe to a broad range of trade and professional journals, these may be things such as:
  - *Current Therapeutics*- Adis International, Locked Bag 280, Frenchs Forest, NSW1640 www.ctonline.com.au This journal normally contains an excellent range of articles from an orthodox medical perspective.
  - *International Clinical Nutrition Review*- Integrated Therapies, PO Box 370, Manly, NSW, 1655. An outstanding monthly review of articles from mainstream journals pertaining to nutrition.

- *Australian Journal of Pharmacy-* Suite F2, 1-15 Barr St, Balmain, NSW, 2041 www.appco.com.au For a monthly view of the industry from a pharmacy perspective.
- *Townsend Letter for Doctors and Patients-* 911 Tyler St, Port Townsend, WA, 98368-6541, USA. www.tldp.com Provides a review of non-medical healthcare research, and carries a good range of well researched articles on most mainstream non-medical healthcare modalities.
- *Australian Journal of Medical Herbalism-* National Herbalists Association, PO Box 61, Broadway, NSW, 2007. One may have to join the Association to receive this, but it carries very well written reviews and original articles on herbal medicine.
- *Journal of the Australian Traditional Medicine Society-* ATMS, PO Box 1027, Meadowbank, NSW 2114. One may have to join the Society to receive this, but it also carries a broad range of well written articles on a broad range on non-medical health topics, as well as providing useful reviews of articles from other journals and insights into political aspects of the industry.
- *Homeopathy* (formerly the British Journal of Homoeopathy)- Journals Marketing Dept, Elsevier Science, 32 Jamestown Rd London, NW1, 7BY, UK www.harcourt-international.com/journals/homp Provides excellent reviews of articles on homoeopathic research and practice from other journals and carries very well written original articles on these two subjects.
- Submit articles for publication in the above journals.
- Maintain an interest in research that relates to one's profession.
- Teach one's chosen modality at local educational institutions.
- Become involved in Internet discussion groups that relate to one's chosen modality.
- Undertake regular training courses in one's chosen field, as well as areas such as computing and marketing.
- Join local commerce associations.

In addition to this, try to avoid having gaps in your clinic bookings. Watching the clock while one waits for the next client carries significant potential for depression- five clients booked back to back in the middle of the day are much easier to deal with than two in the morning and three at the end of the day.

Apart from the activities mentioned above, one of the most important means of maintaining interest and enthusiasm is to take an active if not vigorous interest in one or more things that have absolutely nothing to do with one's chosen profession. This may be anything from stamp collecting through to skydiving, but without such a counterpoint, one may lose the perspective that's essential for enthusiasm, and more importantly, the ability to relate to one's clients as friends and fellows. Enthusiasm is also infectious- once one has it, it can be easily spread, and when it's associated with you or your clinic, it benefits everyone.

Skills Maintenance
Keeping Up
One doesn't need to look too hard at the medical libraries around the country to realise that medical research, particularly research into non-medical therapies, is growing at a startling rate. Keeping up with it can be a full time job, and may be impossible for someone in full time practice, but one should endeavour to do this as much as one can. Fortunately, resources exist that allow easy access to summary versions of such research. Journals concentrating on nutrition such as the International Journal of Clinical Nutrition, herbal journals such as Australian Journal of Medical Herbalism and Planta Medica, homoeopathic journals such as Homoeopathy, and many of the Traditional Chinese Medicine, chiropractic, osteopathic and bodywork journals contain summaries of relevant recent research.

Regular use of searchable Internet database services such as Medline (www.ncbi.nlm.nih.gov/PubMed/) can also be used to search for abstracts of relevant peer reviewed journal articles. Software such as Hyperhealth (contact Hyperhealth, 20 Napier St Fitzroy Vic 3065, Ph/ Fax 03 94172567, www.yulan.com.au/hh) contains excellent searchable databases on natural products and ailments, and are normally updated annually.

Diversifying
It's entirely possible to concentrate too much on one's preferred modality. To do so takes attention away from other types of therapy that can be of great benefit to one's clients. To pursue a course of study in complementary therapies can provide significant benefits not only to clients but also to the depth of understanding of one's principal modality. For the homoeopath, it may be of benefit to monitor developments in the area of nutritional therapy. The acupuncturist can derive great benefit from the study of homoeopathy. The chiropractor or osteopath can learn much from the study of applied kineseology, and the herbalist from pharmacology.

One should keep abreast of the other areas that have an impact on the functioning of the clinic. Developments in the fields of marketing, information technology, management practice and the areas that relate to financial management should also be monitored. Specialist magazines and journals, commercial associations, and the financial press can all be rich sources of information on these subjects.

The Last Word

Finally, it should be kept in mind that success is largely a matter of attitude. As with most things, form tends to follow function, and success will be attracted to those who think and act like successful people. With the appropriate skills, commitment, and the necessary systems, strategies and monitoring processes in place, and one's goals always in focus, success will inevitably be attracted to people who plan for it, and have the capacity to accommodate it. It is the authors hope that you are one of those people.

The Business of Healing

Index